CRITICAL ESSAYS ON

PHILIP LARKIN: THE POEMS

Editors:
Linda Cookson
Bryan Loughrey

LONGMAN
LITERATURE
GUIDES

Longman Literature Guides

Editors: Linda Cookson and Bryan Loughrey

Titles in the series:

CONTENTS

PREFACE

Like all professional groups, literary critics have developed their own specialised language. This is not necessarily a bad thing. Sometimes complex concepts can only be described in a terminology far removed from everyday speech. Academic jargon, however, creates an unnecessary barrier between the critic and the intelligent but less practised reader.

This danger is particularly acute where scholarly books and articles are re-packaged for a student audience. Critical anthologies, for example, often contain extracts from longer studies originally written for specialists. Deprived of their original context, these passages can puzzle and at times mislead. The essays in this volume, however, are all specially commissioned, self-contained works, written with the needs of students firmly in mind.

This is not to say that the contributors — all experienced critics and teachers — have in any way attempted to simplify the complexity of the issues with which they deal. On the contrary, they explore the central problems of the text from a variety of critical perspectives, reaching conclusions which are challenging and at times mutually contradictory.

They try, however, to present their arguments in direct, accessible language and to work within the limitations of scope and length which students inevitably face. For this reason, essays are generally rather briefer than is the practice; they address quite specific topics; and, in line with examination requirements, they incorporate precise textual detail into the body of the discussion.

They offer, therefore, working examples of the kind of essay-writing skills which students themselves are expected to develop. Their diversity, however, should act as a reminder that in the field of literary studies there is no such thing as a 'model' answer. Good essays are the outcome of a creative engagement with literature, of sensitive, attentive reading and careful thought. We hope that those contained in this volume will encourage students to return to the most important starting point of all, the text itself, with renewed excitement and the determination to explore more fully their own critical responses.

How to use this volume

Obviously enough, you should start by reading the text in question. The one assumption that all the contributors make is that you are already familiar with this. It would be helpful, of course, to have read further — perhaps other works by the same author or by influential contemporaries. But we don't assume that you have yet had the opportunity to do this and any references to historical background or to other works of literature are explained.

You should, perhaps, have a few things to hand. It is always a good idea to keep a copy of the text nearby when reading critical studies. You will almost certainly want to consult it when checking the context of quotations or pausing to consider the validity of the critic's interpretation. You should also try to have access to a good dictionary, and ideally a copy of a dictionary of literary terms as well. The contributors have tried to avoid jargon and to express themselves clearly and directly. But inevitably there will be occasional words or phrases with which you are unfamiliar. Finally, we would encourage you to make notes, summarising not just the argument of each essay but also your own responses to what you have read. So keep a pencil and notebook at the ready.

Suitably equipped, the best thing to do is simply begin with whichever topic most interests you. We have deliberately organised each volume so that the essays may be read in any order. One consequence of this is that, for the sake of clarity and self-containment, there is occasionally a degree of overlap between essays. But at least you are not forced to follow one — fairly arbitrary — reading sequence.

Each essay is followed by brief 'Afterthoughts', designed to highlight points of critical interest. But remember, these are only there to remind you that it is *your* responsibility to question what you read. The essays printed here are not a series of 'model' answers to be slavishly imitated and in no way should they be regarded as anything other than a guide or stimulus for your own thinking. We hope for a critically involved response: 'That was interesting. But if *I* were tackling the topic . . .!'

Read the essays in this spirit and you'll pick up many of the skills of critical composition in the process. We have, however, tried to provide more explicit advice in 'A practical guide to essay writing'. You may find this helpful, but do not imagine it offers any magic formulas. The quality of your essays ultimately depends on the quality of your engagement with literary texts. We hope this volume spurs you on to read these with greater understanding and to explore your responses in greater depth.

Andrew Gibson

Andrew Gibson is a Lecturer in English at the University of London and writes both fiction and criticism. His latest academic publication is Reading Narrative Discourse: Studies in the Novel from Cervantes to Beckett

ESSAY

Larkin and ordinariness

Larkin cast himself as a resolutely ordinary and unpretentious poet. For many years, he worked as Librarian at Hull University, leading a life, he said, that was 'as simple' as he could make it.[1] He repeatedly asserted that good poetry was simple and straightforward. He thought, for instance, that Thomas Hardy was a great poet partly because 'his work contains little in thought or reference that needs elucidation, his language is unambiguous, his themes easily comprehensible' (p. 168). On the other hand, Larkin saw the major 'modernists' — Joyce, Eliot, Pound — as having produced a wilfully obscure and esoteric art. Their work was inaccessible to 'anyone with normal vision' (p. 72). Larkin set his face against this trend in modern literature. He allied himself with poets like Hardy and John Betjeman, who seemed to have understood that poetry 'is an affair of sanity, of seeing things as they are' (p. 197). They addressed 'matters of common concern', Larkin thought, in a language common to all (p. 187). He saw himself, too, as establishing 'a direct relation' with the ordinary reading public (p. 129). He refused to address what he called 'professional

---

[1] Philip Larkin, *Required Writing: Miscellaneous Pieces 1955–1982* (London, 1983), p. 57. Throughout this essay, when page numbers are given, they refer to this book.

readers', the dons and their students (p. 252). Indeed, he sought partly to ally himself with a larger public against the professionals. Like most ordinary people, he had serious misgivings about literary folk, and the value of the literary life. 'Books are a load of crap' he once described as a sentiment 'to which every bosom returns an echo' (p. 48). In a deliberate display of a sort of willed lack of intellect, he even said that he 'adored' Mrs Thatcher (p. 52).

Larkin is thus an anti-intellectual poet. He refused to 'jack himself up' to 'a concept of poetry' lying outside his own and other people's lives (p. 175). He said, for instance, that in 'writing about unhappiness' he was simply writing about the lives of 'most people' (p. 47). He argued that the poet is 'really engaged in recreating the familiar' (p. 55). His poetry matches a concern with familiar things with a startlingly familiar language. Many of his poems are strewn with vulgar idioms and slang phrases. So, too, the Larkin presented within the poetry is often a very ordinary figure. We catch him 'Groping back to bed after a piss' in 'Sad Steps' (*High Windows*), for instance; or awkwardly unhooking his cycle-clips and furtively donating an Irish sixpence in 'Church Going' (*The Less Deceived*). Larkin has a very good feel for what is both commonplace and immediate. No poet has better described the pouring of a gin and tonic ('Sympathy in White Major', *High Windows*). But his 'common touch' also has more important effects. Quite a few of the poems operate reductively. They convey nuggets of 'modern wisdom' in clear and comprehensible form. Filtered through Larkin, for example, post-Freudian knowingness becomes the famous assertion that 'They fuck you up, your mum and dad' ('This Be The Verse', *High Windows*). Poems like 'This Be The Verse' seem partly to emerge out of an impulse to share. Larkin did in fact write a lot of good poems about ordinary, shared experience — disappointment and the prospect of death, for instance, as in 'Next, Please' (*The Less Deceived*), or the ugliness of ageing, as in 'Skin' (*The Less Deceived*). He repeatedly adopts the first person plural in his poetry. It reflects his desire to speak on behalf of all. Some of his best and most sensitive poems forge bonds with others by identifying with ordinariness, or bestowing value upon it. Thus 'To the Sea' (*High Windows*), for instance, ends with a moving tribute to the ordinary, clumsy men and women at the beach who patiently continue to teach their children and help the old. It may be they, the poet says, who ultimately 'do best'. Similarly, 'Mr Bleaney' (*The Whitsun Weddings*) very effectively conveys the pathetic near-nullity of Mr Bleaney's circumstances. Both poems display that rather distanced compassion that is characteristic of some of Larkin's best verse.

But there was another side to Larkin. Part of him cultivated the image of a plain, ordinary, insular Englishman, seemingly indifferent, for example, to literature in languages other than English. But he can also be found quoting in German, and alluding to French and German writers like Villon, Schopenhauer, Proust and Montherlant. If he cast himself as an unpretentious anti-modernist, Larkin also thought he resembled Dylan Thomas, and refers approvingly to the (notably obscure) work of the modern poet Wallace Stevens. He praised a poetry that could be understood 'first go', but he also deplored it, at times (*Required Writing*, pp. 61,293). Certainly, he thought highly of John Betjeman as a poet 'who restored direct intelligible communication' (p. 217). But he also liked him, not because he was ordinary, but because Betjeman's was 'a mind of extraordinary originality'. No one else's 'remotely' resembled it (p. 206). Larkin insisted that poets ought to keep in touch with ordinary people. But his articles and reviews were also particularly sensitive to poets at odds with the world: A E Housman, for instance, whose nature made him 'one set apart' (p. 264); Francis Thompson, incapable of any adequate 'recognition of reality' (p. 120); W H Davies, who was willing to sacrifice all ordinary satisfactions to poetry; Edward Thomas, 'to whom no hardship or humiliation' outweighed 'the romance of scraping a living from the printed word' (p. 189). Larkin writes very well, too, of poets, like Stevie Smith and Emily Dickinson, who seem to him to combine the simple and the strange in their verse. That isn't surprising. Larkin may have found Hardy's strength partly in his simplicity. But he saw his own poems as solutions 'to a complex pressure of needs' (p. 76). He wrote them, he said, to preserve what was essentially a 'composite and complex experience' (p. 79).

Something rare and fine, then, was tucked away beneath Larkin's bluffness and plainness. He played it down of course, but that only draws added attention to it in the writing. Larkin once wrote of Wilfred Owen that he 'found it difficult to come to terms with the world through the usual channels' (p. 232). His own poetry frequently suggests that he could have described himself in the same way. Certainly, he saw himself as an 'outsider', partly just because he stayed a bachelor (p. 65). Plenty of Larkin's poems are about alienation from the common world. In 'Spring' (*The Less Deceived*), for example, the poet is an 'indigestible sterility', one of those spring itself 'has least use for'. 'Wants' (*The Less Deceived*) is about 'the wish to be alone', and the subsequent turn away from the ordinary human world. 'Maiden Name' (*The Less Deceived*) is partly about resisting the usual pattern of experience, and 'Dry-Point' (*The Less Deceived*) is partly about wanting more than human beings normally get. Occasionally, Larkin's poetry shows some distaste for commonplace humanity — for the 'cut-price crowd' in 'Here' (*The Whitsun Weddings*), for example, and the women whose 'thick tongue blort' in 'Faith Healing' (*The Whitsun Weddings*). But Larkin can also seem acutely nostalgic for ordinariness, as something beyond his reach. Far from consistently 'recreating the familiar', Larkin sometimes seems much more interested in robbing it of its familiarity, and making it seem strange. In 'Broadcast' (*The Whitsun Weddings*), for instance, the woman loses her familiarity and becomes remote, dwarfed by the circumstances and the music, mere 'hands, tiny in all that air, applauding'. He is fascinated by moments which completely change our perceptions of the ordinary, as in 'Ambulances' (*The Whitsun Weddings*). Some of the poems — like 'Whatever Happened?' (*The Less Deceived*) — reveal a Larkin intrigued by the psychology of ordinariness. It intrigues him precisely because it isn't his own kind of psychology.

For that matter, in a poem like 'To the Sea', it is because he feels separate and outside ordinary life that Larkin can make it seem positive. After all, ordinary people don't see themselves as embodying the value of ordinariness. They're too ordinary to bother, and too busy leading ordinary lives. Alienation from the familiar, then, helps Larkin to appreciate it better. But it also takes him in the opposite direction. It draws him to things outside the confines of the busy, common world: 'unfenced existence', for instance, 'untalkative, out of reach', at the end of

'Here'; the remote room, in the last stanza of 'Dry-Point'; the horses that have even 'slipped their names' in 'At Grass' (*The Less Deceived*); most of all, perhaps, the 'high windows' in the poem of that name (*High Windows*). Larkin keeps on returning to an empty, bare, soundless and lonely world. He's attracted to wastelands that are strewn with scrub and debris; to people and things on the outskirts or margins (like Hull), or left behind in the hurry forwards; to what is 'natural' and 'fouled-up', as opposed to the new, glossy and get-ahead ('Posterity', *High Windows*); to places where 'leaves unnoticed thicken,/ Hidden weeds flower, neglected waters quicken' ('Here'). 'In a time of global concepts,' Larkin wrote, Betjeman insisted on 'the little, the forgotten, the unprofitable, the obscure.' If the spirit of our century 'is onwards, outwards and upwards, the spirit of Betjeman's work is backwards, inwards and downwards' (*Required Writing*, p. 208). Larkin's own work is imbued with a similar 'spirit'. In a similar way, it defies the most common trends in Larkin's culture.

So, like Owen again, as Larkin himself described him, Larkin begins to emerge as a 'complicated, and even contradictory, personality: commonplace yet uniquely gifted' (p. 238). In some respects, he was committed to being ordinary. But he also possessed certain qualities — delicacies of feeling, for instance — that pulled him away from ordinariness. They weren't really at all compatible with it. The different Larkins repeatedly struggle with each other in the poems. This is reflected in the number of poems that work by contrasting two particular kinds of thought or feeling. The poet may appear to take sides in such poems. But he also often leaves his case looking shaky, or even ironically compromised. Take 'Toads', for instance, or 'Reasons for Attendance', 'Poetry of Departures' (*The Less Deceived*), 'Nothing to be Said', 'Self's the Man'. 'Dockery and Son', 'Send no Money' (*The Whitsun Weddings*), 'Money', 'High Windows' and 'Vers de Société' (*High Windows*). All of these poems involve a conflict between more and less commonplace attitudes and ways of life. One such conflict comes across particularly clearly in 'Born Yesterday' (*The Less Deceived*), a poem written for the infant Sally Amis. May you have all the gifts others have wished you, Larkin tells the baby. But if they don't come your way, then 'may you be ordinary':

Have, like other women,
An average of talents:
Not ugly, not good-looking,
Nothing uncustomary
To pull you off your balance,
That, unworkable itself,
Stops all the rest from working.
In fact, may you be dull —
If that is what a skilled,
Vigilant, flexible,
Unemphasised, enthralled
Catching of happiness is called.

On the surface, the point is clear. Better be commonplace, Larkin is saying, than have some odd streak in your personality that makes life difficult and unprofitable. But the reader may wonder why the poet piles up so long and exquisite a selection of adjectives in the last four lines. Well, they partly suggest that the 'happiness' at issue may be a very subtle and elusive affair. That makes us ask awkward questions about how likely Sally Amis (or anyone else) is to 'catch' it. But at the same time the lines are wonderfully expressive. Nothing could be less dull than this particular statement of the value of dullness. So there's a final paradox: the poet and poem seem to have less and less in common with the quality they praise. It may be much better not to be unusual. But the talent that is trying to persuade us of the point, here, is pretty unusual itself.

Many of Larkin's poems revolve around this kind of paradox. We seem to have reached the kind of conclusion that literary critics are often fond of: Larkin's attitudes to ordinariness are 'ambiguous'. Actually, though, I think Larkin is interested in something slightly different to 'ambiguities in meaning'. Let's look at two of his favourite concerns. The first is *perspective*. Larkin has always recognised that perspectives are multiple. He begins one of his pieces on jazz, for instance, with a quotation from Schopenhauer: 'Every man mistakes the limits of his own vision for the limits of the world' (*Required Writing*, p. 309). Perceptions differ, in other words, and everyone takes their own perception for truth. But Larkin himself is rather good at avoiding this 'mistake'. He said he couldn't have been a satirist — 'you have to think you know better than everyone else. I've never done that.' (p. 73). As a jazz critic, he insisted that his ear was 'not the only ear' (p. 298). As a reviewer, he recognised that his own notions were never 'absolute and unchallengeable' (p. 302). So, too, as a poet, he is always interested in shifts of perspective. There are perspectives in time, for instance. In 'Reference Back' (*The Whitsun Weddings*) Larkin himself refers to 'the long perspectives' in time that are 'Open at each instant of our lives'. 'Such perspectives have the power to shock us out of our habitual, commonplace sense of ourselves and where we belong. Various of Larkin's poems are about this sort of shock — 'Maiden Name', 'Lines on a Young Lady's Photograph Album', 'I Remember, I Remember', 'Triple Time' (*The Less Deceived*), 'Reference Back' and 'Love Songs in Age' (*The Whitsun Weddings*), 'Annus Mirabilis' (*High Windows*). As we'll see in a moment, it's at the centre of 'High Windows'. Larkin also looks at the (often world-sized) differences between other forms of perspective. 'Livings' (*High Windows*) deals with very different views of things engendered by different kinds of life. 'For Sidney Bechet' (*The Whitsun Weddings*) looks at the different 'appropriate falsehoods' awoken by Bechet's music. 'The Whitsun Weddings' is very conscious of what the different faces on the platforms 'define' as 'departing' from them. Such poems move between more and less usual forms of understanding. They remind us of the relative value of different angles of vision. They also underline the relative nature of ordinariness itself.

The second of Larkin's 'favourite concerns' I want just briefly to look at is deprivation. Larkin has always been fascinated by impoverishment, loss, closeness to nullity. Many of his poems teeter on the edge of 'the solving emptiness/ That lies just under all we do' ('Ambulances', *The Whitsun Weddings*). There are some ordinary examples. In 'The Old Fools' (*High Windows*), for instance, Larkin imagines what life might be like for those who are old and close to death. 'Ignorance' (*The Whitsun Weddings*) deals with 'knowing nothing', never being sure of 'what is true or right or real'. The deprivation in other poems, however, seems anything but ordinary. It is harder to define, and sometimes willed, rather than inflicted. There is the exposure to a world coming up like 'a cold sun' at the end of

'No Road' (*The Less Deceived*), for instance. There is the strange, exhilarated delight in the 'hollows' of sea and the 'lit-up galleries' of sky at the end of 'Absences' (*The Less Deceived*) — 'Such attics cleared of me! Such absences!' This last is revealing. Larkin once said that deprivation was for him 'what daffodils were for Wordsworth' (*Required Writing*, p. 47). Now for Wordsworth, the daffodils of the poem weren't just subject-matter or 'inspiration'. They were a source of 'gaiety' and 'glee'. The memory of them was a pleasure and a comfort in solitude. So Larkin doesn't just mean that deprivation is one of his central themes. Oddly enough, he's saying that, however chilling, deprivation, for him, can be strangely elating and sustaining. It is a means to possible vision; an escape from the ordinary world, or an antidote to it.

I want to go back, now, to the poems in which we noticed a quarrel between different Larkins. Here, as we saw, the ordinary point of view both challenges the unusual one, and is challenged by it. But the most important consequence of this is not 'ambiguity'. The two perspectives don't just clash, but tend to neutralise each other. Thus 'Reasons for Attendance' (*The Less Deceived*) leaves us quite unsure of whose point of view to credit: the sex-oriented couples', or the art-oriented poet's. In 'Self's the Man' (*The Whitsun Weddings*), similarly, Larkin finally undercuts his own attempt to look down on Arnold from an elevated position of stoical superiority. Whose choice of life should we praise or prefer? The poet simply won't say. So, too, 'Dockery and Son' (*The Whitsun Weddings*) levels out the differences between its two alternatives. By the end of the poem, Dockery's and Larkin's lives both seem to amount to more or less the same thing. 'Vers de Société' (*High Windows*) swings indecisively from one view to the opposite, from the value of solitude to the value of company. All of these poems avoid the mistake referred to by Schopenhauer. In fact, Larkin plays off 'limited visions' against each other. Ordinariness has limitations. So do attempts to ignore or reject it. Larkin lets the two opposed attitudes erode each other. But we're therefore left deprived of either (or any) conviction. We lose a sense of the better course in life, and even the confidence that there clearly is such a thing. We lose certainty, and even the sense of clarity and definition.

In both his prose and his poetry, Larkin continually returns to what we might call the challenge of otherness. He's continually imagining other attitudes to life. In poem after poem — however briefly — he ponders another person's way of seeing or being. As he does so, it starts to weaken his hold on his own. It can even unsettle his certainty of having a view at all. Finally, it may deprive him of the very foundations of self. But for Larkin, that is not necessarily a negative experience. Loss of self is something he associated with the poet's calling. 'I didn't choose poetry,' he said. 'Poetry chose me' (*Required Writing*, p. 62). More important still, he can also associate loss or absence of self with exhilaration or vision, as in 'Absences', or 'Going' (*The Less Deceived*). As perspectives in his poems annul each other, then, a kind of release becomes possible. It's partly just a release from the ordinary world. Larkin has repeatedly been fascinated by the image of 'sun-comprehending glass' in which 'any-angled light' can 'congregate endlessly' ('High Windows' (*High Windows*), 'Water', *The Whitsun Weddings*). It is an image of something remote from the ordinary, and, for Larkin, it has an almost religious significance. The endings of many of his poems are, in a way, like miniature, imperfect versions of this image. For they allow different 'angles' on things to co-exist. That's both a sort of deprivation, and — for Larkin — potentially uplifting. We might turn now, finally, to 'High Windows'. For, where other Larkin poems often tend to leave us on the threshold, 'High Windows' takes us over it. It's a poem that's important for understanding Larkin, partly because we get the pattern, here, in a peculiarly classic form:

> When I see a couple of kids
> And guess he's fucking her and she's
> Taking pills or wearing a diaphragm,
> I know this is paradise
>
> Everyone old has dreamed of all their lives —
> Bonds and gestures pushed to one side
> Like an outdated combine harvester,
> And everyone young going down the long slide
>
> To happiness, endlessly. I wonder if
> Anyone looked at me, forty years back,

And thought, *That'll be the life*;
No God any more, or sweating in the dark

About hell and that, or having to hide
What you think of the priest. He
And his lot will all go down the long slide
Like free bloody birds.

We start with Larkin's own 'perspective' on the 'kids' apparently enjoying their sex-lives. His view of them is a mixture of irony, disenchantment, unease, awe, even envy. The kids' world, he suggests, may after all be paradise. But he also wavers. Isn't it merely what others — especially the old — imagine to be a kind of paradise? The idea pushes Larkin into reversing perspectives. When young themselves, didn't those who are elderly now present the same challenge and threat to their elders? And didn't the resentment of the old, then, have as much and as little reason behind it as now? Such feelings only ever have a relative value and importance, the poem says. It starts to shade into futility; an awareness of the pointlessness and nullity of such ordinary concerns. But then, suddenly, the movement towards loss and emptiness becomes profoundly liberating:

And immediately

Rather than words comes the thought of high windows:
The sun-comprehending glass,
And beyond it, the deep blue air, that shows
Nothing, and is nowhere, and is endless.

These closing lines seem inconsequential. But the inconsequence is partly what makes the point. The poet has imagined two sets of attitudes, and then let them collapse, and logic with them. With that collapse comes a sense of deprivation, but also a spontaneous, irrational sense of freedom. It's a freedom from the ordinary world, and also from the uneasy sense of not quite belonging to the ordinary world. For it's not impossible that — for Larkin, at least — there was something that might matter more than either.

AFTERTHOUGHTS

1

Do you agree that Larkin is 'an anti-intellectual poet' (page 10)?

2

What do you understand by 'Quite a few of his poems operate reductively' (page 10)?

3

How far do you agree with Larkin's own view that his poetry embodied a 'composite and complex experience' (page 11)?

4

What paradoxes does Gibson identify in this essay in Larkin's attitude to ordinariness?

Cedric Watts

Cedric Watts is Professor of English at Sussex University, and author of many scholarly publications.

ESSAY

Larkin and jazz

Philip Larkin became a jazz fan while at school in the 1930s. He persuaded his parents to buy him a drum kit and, at concerts, would sit where he could best observe the drummer's technique. Gradually he relinquished his ambition to become a drummer, but the enthusiasm for jazz remained with him all his life. The most obvious literary consequences of this enthusiasm were the book *All What Jazz* and a few poems in which this music is specified. There may, however, have been subtler and more extensive connections between jazz and Larkin's literary output. In this essay, Part 1 discusses the book; Part 2 discusses a trio of poems; and Part 3 briefly considers those larger connections.

1

Between 1961 and 1968 Larkin reviewed jazz records for the *Daily Telegraph*. Eventually these reviews were collected and republished as the volume *All What Jazz: A Record Diary 1961–68* (London, 1970); and this book contained an Introduction which has since gained some notoriety.

That Introduction begins innocuously enough. Larkin tells

how, in schooldays and at Oxford, he nurtured an enjoyment of jazz, its rhythms, distinctive voices and improvised power: Louis Armstrong, Bessie Smith, Jimmy Noone and others provided an education of which school lessons had provided no glimpse; and this interest promoted a shared communion between Larkin and his friends — a musical freemasonry: 'For us, jazz became part of the private joke of existence . . .'.

In the 1950s, the long-playing record was introduced; instead of rejoicing, Larkin 'was suspicious of it' as 'it seemed a package deal, forcing you to buy bad tracks along with good at an unwantedly-high price'. The same period also saw a great revival of jazz in Britain: traditional jazz by Humphrey Lyttelton and Chris Barber led the way; for a time it enjoyed unprecedented commercial success; and, again, Larkin says that he distrusted this phase: 'there seemed an element of slightly-unreal archaism about much of the trad of the period.' This was the time when American modern jazz (pioneered by Dizzy Gillespie, Charlie Parker and Thelonius Monk) became widely known and imitated in Great Britain: 'What I heard on the wireless seemed singularly unpromising,' Larkin comments.

What is already remarkable, within the first few pages of the book, is the narrow, inflexible, embattled basis of Larkin's enthusiasm; a quality of nostalgic purism generating remark-able distrust of developments which many jazz fans at the time regarded with delight. Why, then, did Larkin agree to be the *Daily Telegraph*'s regular reviewer of jazz records? He gives two reasons. First, he thought that if he listened to enough of 'the new stuff', he would come to enjoy it; and second, 'I hadn't really any intention of being a jazz *critic*':

> In literature, I understood, there were several old whores who had grown old in the reviewing game by praising everything, and I planned to be their jazz equivalent.

But when the packages of records arrived, he found to his dismay (he says) that the more he listened to modern jazz, the more he detested it; to him it was not really jazz at all. Gillespie, Parker and Monk were bad enough, but with 'Miles Davis and John Coltrane a new inhumanity emerged', and after 'Coltrane, of course all was chaos, hatred and absurdity'. At last, Larkin explains, he recognised what had gone wrong: jazz, like literature and art, had become contaminated by modernism. Just as Ezra Pound and James Joyce had changed the course of literature by subverting tradition and as Picasso and Matisse had revolutionised painting, so the modern jazz musicians had rebelled against their heritage and pursued mystifying experimentation:

> I dislike such things not because they are new, but because they are irresponsible exploitations of technique in contradiction of human life as we know it. This is my essential criticism of modernism, whether perpetrated by Parker, Pound or Picasso: it helps us neither to enjoy nor to endure. It will divert us as long as we are prepared to be mystified or outraged, but maintains its hold only by being more mystifying and hence more outrageous; it has no lasting power. Hence the compulsion on every modernist to wade deeper and deeper into violence and obscenity: hence the succession of Parker by Rollins and Coltrane, and of Rollins and Coltrane by Coleman, Ayler and Shepp. In a way, it's a relief: if jazz records are to be long one screech [sic], if painting is to be a blank canvas, if a play is to be two hours of sexual intercourse performed *coram populo* [in public], then let's get it over, the sooner the better, in the hope that human values will then be free to reassert themselves.

After this bitter polemic against the whole of modern jazz and the whole of modernism — a movement which embraces most of the distinguished innovators in twentieth-century culture, and a movement to which Larkin's own poetry inevitably owes some debts — Larkin's tone changes. He says that he hopes that the reviews themselves 'are tolerably free from such polemics': 'I tried in writing them to be fair and conscientious, and there was many a time when I substituted "challenging" for "insolent", "adventurous" for "excruciating", and "colourful" for "viciously absurd" . . .'.

So a huge paradox begins to emerge. When Larkin writes frankly and apparently sincerely, the result is a sweeping denunciation of modernism including all modern jazz. Yet, in the actual reviews, Larkin writes predominantly in a much more considerate and scrupulous way: here he is 'fair and conscientious'. Furthermore, by an obvious literary test — stylistic acuteness — the 'conscientious' Larkin seems to be a better and more intelligent critic than the 'sincere' Larkin. Thus we may learn that sincerity is no criterion of merit (since a sincerely bad man is no less bad for being sincere) and that, in Larkin's case, the discipline of striving to write fairly may actually have liberated more of his intelligence than did the freedom he enjoyed in that Introduction. I'll give a few illustrations of this.

In the Introducion, Larkin says that the music of Charlie Parker and his associates was 'pinched, unhappy, febrile'; Parker was 'compulsively fast and showy', with a tone 'thin and sometimes shrill'. But now hear Larkin as, in a review dated 10 June 1961, he describes the Gillespie-Parker concert taped at Carnegie Hall in 1947:

> Listening to Parker, one has the impression of a man who not only could translate his ideas into notes at superhuman speed, but who was simultaneously aware of half a dozen ways of resolving any given musical situation, and could somehow refer to all of them in passing beyond it. In his extended solos in 'Groovin' High' and 'Confirmation' idea succeeds idea so unhesitatingly and at such high pressure that the hearer acquits him of any premeditated desire to astonish. Clearly, his only problem was how to get it out fast enough.
>
> This is important, because the new modern jazz that Parker and Gillespie founded was in part a reaction against the ossified platitudes of 1940 big-band jazz which they were both forced to play. Driven to exasperation by the fag-end of the swing era, they and a few other young Negro musicians produced a music among themselves that was technically, melodically and rhythmically beyond their elders and their audience alike. By doing so, they recaptured for their race the jazz initiative, and, incidentally, split the world of this music into two camps. But on the evidence of these solos alone it would be absurd to call Parker's music a reaction. As well call a leaping salmon a reaction.

'As well call a leaping salmon a reaction': a finely appropriate image to be relished by anyone who enjoys jazz and appreciates Parker. What's more, the account offered here not only of Parker's style but also of the circumstances of his emergence is altogether more fair than the jaundiced account given in the

Introduction. Again, the reviews of Miles Davis, while offering frank acknowledgement of Larkin's distaste for much of his work, still contain finely phrased appreciations. Of one LP he remarks:

> The slow Davis solos ... are declaimed with enormous authority, keen and kingly, like incidental music of genius for a Swedish film of *Hamlet* ... Davis is his usual bleak self, his notes wilting at the edges as if with frost ...

If you know the more plangent, melancholy Davis solos of the 1960s, you'll recognise the precision of Larkin's remark about notes 'wilting at the edges as if with frost'. D H Lawrence once said, 'Never trust the artist. Trust the tale.' Often the tale told by Larkin's reviews seems more trustworthy than the crusty personal polemic which dominates their Introduction. Nevertheless, the last paragraph of that Introduction has a related ambivalence which generates one of Larkin's most interesting poems — a work that has been largely unappreciated, precisely because it's a poem in prose.

In that final paragraph, Larkin tries to imagine the readers of his reviews. First the tone is glumly sardonic: 'I imagine them, sullen fleshy inarticulate men, stockbrokers, sellers of goods ... husbands of ageing and bitter wives ... fathers of cold-eyed lascivious daughters on the pill ...'. But then, in the last few lines, the tone modulates from the sardonic to the melancholy, and we hear that soured romanticism, that sad recognition of ageing and loss, which re-echoes in Larkin's verses. Those readers, he reflects, are:

> men in whom a pile of scratched coverless 78s in the attic can awaken memories of vomiting blindly from small Tudor windows to Muggsy Spanier's 'Sister Kate', or winding up a gramophone in a punt to play Armstrong's 'Body and Soul'; men whose first coronary is coming like Christmas; who drift, loaded helplessly with commitments and obligations and other necessary observances, into the darkening avenues of age and incapacity, deserted by everything that once made life sweet. These I have tried to remind of the excitement of jazz, and tell where it may still be found.

From 'men whose first coronary' to 'everything that once made life sweet', as the rhythm of the sentence rolls and slows to its close, we hear the familiar tones of so many of Larkin's dourly disconsolate poems. Having begun the long description by thinking of the readers as prosperous middle-aged stockbrokers, alien strangers encumbered with families, Larkin has ended by thinking of the readers as (since they, for all their sins, are fellow jazz fans) men like himself. The result is a prose-poem in which glum scorn has modulated into a melancholy which is perilously close to a vicarious self-pity.

2

Of the verse-poems in which jazz is prominent, 'Reasons for Attendance' (in *The Less Deceived*) invokes 'The trumpet's voice, loud and authoritative' from 'that lifted, rough-tongued bell/ (Art, if you like)'. The poem's narrator depicts himself as a person who, from outside, watches through a window young people dancing to the music. They, he reflects, may think that 'happiness is found by couples' — 'sheer/ Inaccuracy, as far as I'm concerned'; he is attracted by the jazz, an individual voice reassuring him of his own individuality:

> Therefore I stay outside,
> Believing this; and they maul to and fro,
> Believing that; and both are satisfied,
> If no one has misjudged himself. Or lied.

It's a wry, credibly qualified ending: perhaps both the couples and the solitary hearer may be deceived. The phrase 'Or lied' converts into a strength what had previously seemed a weakness of the poem, the crude contrast between, on one side, the eavesdropper presented as an appreciator of jazz and individualism, and, on the other side, the young couples seen as intent on sexual happiness. The 'Or lied' draws attention to the quite credible possibility that the lonely observer has been partly jealous of the young people (hadn't he spoken of 'The wonderful feel of girls'?). Indeed, the meaning and strength of the poem gains in proportion to the range of the imputed lying. What needs to be questioned is the too-facile contrast between the sensitive lonely observer on the outside and the supposedly less sensitive gregarious young people on the inside; the poem's final phrase does much, though perhaps not enough, to question that contrast.

'Reference Back' (in *The Whitsun Weddings*) pays tribute to King Oliver's 'Riverside Blues', recorded in 1923. The narrator says that when, in the 1950s, he was playing the record in his 'unsatisfactory room' at home, his mother called out 'That was a pretty one' from the hallway. So the incident links 'those antique negroes' who played in Chicago thirty years previously, the narrator now (in his 'unsatisfactory prime'), and his mother downstairs (in her 'unsatisfactory age'). The repetition of 'unsatisfactory' prepares the way for the pessimistic meditations in the final stanza: these chronological conjunctions 'link us to our losses':

> worse,
> They show us what we have as it once was,
> Blindingly undiminished, just as though
> By acting differently we could have kept it so.

The recorded music has endured undiminished through time; but the lives of the hearers fall short of what might have been. To paraphrase the ending of this poem is not easy, because not enough is done by the narrator to justify the predominant melancholy. Just as the repeated 'unsatisfactory' lacks sufficient justification in the text, so that it is a judgement that has to be taken on trust, so the 'worse' in the last few lines seems a wilful judgement; another writer, one imagines, could have made of the same incident — with better justification — a more positive poem in which the emphasis falls on the fact that despite the years, the music remains to be enjoyed, and that both the narrator and his mother are, for a while, in their different ways, linked in enjoyment of it.

The most affirmative and most famous of Larkin's jazz poems is 'For Sidney Bechet' (also in *The Whitsun Weddings*). Larkin's favourite jazz musician was Sidney Bechet, the virtuoso of the soprano saxophone, celebrated for his dextrous technique, passionately vibrant impetus and soaring romanticism of phrase. That tone, the narrator says, awakens dreams or illusions: some hearers may imagine an idyllic Latin Quarter of New Orleans; others may fantasise about the brothel area, the

Storyville where the jazz bands once flourished in the 'sporting houses'. On the narrator, Bechet's music 'falls as they say love should,/Like an enormous yes':

> My Crescent City
> Is where your speech alone is understood,

> And greeted as the natural noise of good,
> Scattering long- haired grief and scored pity.

One weakness of the poem is that word 'scattering' in the last line, which can mean either 'repelling in different directions' or 'distributing in different directions'. The context strongly supports the former sense, but one has to calculate for a while before rejecting the latter sense. Another feature of the poem which will cause readers to form varying judgements of it is that to the jazz fan who knows Bechet's solos and the legends of New Orleans (the Crescent City), the poem's allusions will be clear and its enthusiasm for the music will need no vindication; whereas readers who lack this knowledge will encounter not only a more difficult poem but also one which is hollow at the core: for the poem's centre is provided by memories of that busy, urgent, questing and finally soaring tone of Bechet's saxophone, with its distinctive vibrato and majestic lyricism.

3

Philip Larkin's devotion to jazz had several large consequences. Melancholy and disillusionment came easily to Larkin; the works of Bechet, Armstrong, Bessie Smith and the other jazz-performers whom he admired provided sustenance and hope. They set him examples of creativity that seemed untainted by academia, by pedantry and snobbery. Repeatedly they must have encouraged him to produce poetry which, being both tech-nically adept and emotionally frank (as good jazz is), would communicate itself more readily to readers and hearers than did much of the academically respectable poetry of modern times. Traditional jazz taught Larkin that despondency could be trans-muted by art into affirmation. He never mastered the drums, but he became a wryly intelligent soloist of the blues.

AFTERTHOUGHTS

1

'Sincerity is no criterion of merit' (page 23). Does this hold true for literature?

2

Do you have to enjoy jazz music to appreciate Larkin's poems on jazz musicians?

3

Do you agree that the final phrase of 'Reasons for Attendance' does 'much, though perhaps not enough' (page 26)?

4

What relationship does Watts find between Larkin's jazz criticism and his poetic technique?

Michael Gearin-Tosh

*Michael Gearin-Tosh is Fellow and
Tutor in English Literature at St
Catherine's College, Oxford. He is also
Associate Director of the Oxford School
of Drama.*

ESSAY

Deprivation and love in Larkin's poetry

Larkin is often caricatured, and it was he who started the
process: 'always missing out on sex and happiness, he described
himself in middle age as looking like a balding salmon' recalled
John Cunningham (*Guardian*, 27 September 1988), 'and there
were the outrageous quotes: "Deprivation is for me what
daffodils were to Wordsworth".' Self-caricature and outrageous-
ness are ways of dealing with pain, however; and deprivation
is not the same thing as indifference or stoicism, least of all from
a poet who wrote about love.

'Wedding-Wind' (*The Less Deceived*), an early poem,
explores the rapture of a marriage night:

> The wind blew all my wedding-day,
> And my wedding-night was the night of the high wind
> And a stable door was banging, again and again,
> That he must go and shut it, leaving me
> Stupid in candlelight, hearing rain,
> Seeing my face in the twisted candlestick,
> Yet seeing nothing. When he came back
> He said the horses were restless, and I was sad
> That any man or beast that night should lack
> The happiness I had.

Now in the day
All's ravelled under the sun by the wind's blowing.
He has gone to look at the floods, and I
Carry a chipped pail to the chicken-run,
Set it down, and stare. All is the wind
Hunting through clouds and forests, thrashing
My apron and the hanging cloths on the line.
Can it be borne, this bodying-forth by wind
Of joy my actions turn on, like a thread
Carrying beads? Shall I be let to sleep
Now this perpetual morning shares my bed?
Can even death dry up
These new delighted lakes, conclude
Our kneeling as cattle by all-generous waters?

Larkin also used wind in his first novel, *Jill*, which was written about the same time. John Kemp is elated because Christopher Warner, his charismatic room-mate at Oxford, reveals that Jill has not been seduced as John had feared:

> when he awoke in the morning he felt not despair, but happiness, his mood having changed overnight as the wind might swing completely round. It was only half light when he took his towel and went for a bath, and a few stars were still shining among the towers. Smoke from newly-lit fires poured from chimneys and was whipped away. Wind, warm and blustering, tore along under the overcast sky: in half an hour it would be an ordinary dull morning. But John did not see it like that; this half-light, this standing as it were on a prow coming over the edge of a new day, all seemed to represent the imminence of something new. And what could that be but Jill? The wet green grass in the quadrangle, the brooding of the cloisters, the trees with their dripping twigs, and, above all, the wind — these felt like the agents of some great force that was on his side. He felt sure that he was going to succeed.

(*Jill*, pp. 182–183)

Imminence in *Jill* has become fulfilment in 'Wedding-Wind' where the wind is no longer an 'agent' but a symbol. This enables the otherness of the wind to be played against what the girl desires or can endure. The wind has become fearsomely intimate, not safely observed by John on his way to the comfort of a bath, but 'thrashing' her clothes on the line and, in words which suggest pregnancy, 'borne' and 'bodying-forth'. And the wind has become absolute, almost triumphing over time. In *Jill* after 'half an hour it would be an ordinary dull morning' but the wedding-wind is a symbol of 'perpetual morning'.

Larkin owed a debt to Yeats and also to Shelley when writing in this vein. The turning point of the poem is when the lady sets down her pail and stares. Left alone by the virile 'he', she does not retreat from the presence of the gale although it is daunting: 'All's ravelled' . . . 'All is the wind/ Hunting . . . thrashing'. Instead she gives herself to the wind in meditation and this is marked by the concentration of gaze in her 'stare' (Yeats's word for the concentration of the Chinamen in 'Lapis Lazuli' and the people in 'The Statues'). Her reward is suggested by the image in lines 17–19:

> Can it be borne, this bodying-forth by wind
> Of joy my actions turn on, like a thread
> Carrying beads?

There is a sense of great assurance in this bridge between her and the 'hunting' wind: too exact and human to belittle either, the simile indicates that she has found a point of relationship with the wind's cosmic energy. In doing so, she advances beyond what is so moodily caught in the near rhyme of 'shut it' and 'stupid' in lines 4–5. Then she saw 'nothing' without him. But, aroused and strengthened by the wedding night, she has a new resilience, her love is radiant as 'this perpetual morning' which has replaced the candlelight. Wind dries water but in asking if even death can dry 'these new delighted lakes' she celebrates how, for her, the lovers have moved beyond a world in which 'All is the wind' to one in which love surmounts even the grandeurs of nature.

'Love Songs in Age' (*The Whitsun Weddings*), written some ten years later, shows the development of Larkin's voice:

> She kept her songs, they took so little space,
>   The covers pleased her:
> One bleached from lying in a sunny place,
> One marked in circles by a vase of water,

One mended, when a tidy fit had seized her,
 And coloured, by her daughter —
So they had waited, till in widowhood
She found them, looking for something else, and stood

Relearning how each frank submissive chord
 Had ushered in
Word after sprawling hyphenated word,
And the unfailing sense of being young
Spread out like a spring-woken tree, wherein
 That hidden freshness, sung,
That certainty of time laid up in store
As when she played them first. But, even more,

The glare of that much-mentioned brilliance, love,
 Broke out, to show
Its bright incipience sailing above,
Still promising to solve, and satisfy,
And set unchangeably in order. So
 To pile them back, to cry,
Was hard, without lamely admitting how
It had not done so then, and could not now.

The 'all-generous waters' have been dried not by death or even the wind, but by life: they were a mirage. Yet the poem is not without generosity and it comes from Larkin himself. His theme as he writes in 'Faith Healing' (*The Whitsun Weddings*) is 'all time has disproved' — a theme for a moralist, except that Larkin's understanding and gentleness soften moralising with love. The covers of the songs have the marks of wear and tear, but what they recall in lines 3–6 is pleasurable: a warm sun, flowers in a vase, repairing what you value and a child with crayons. Larkin's brilliant strategy is to make these associations more 'musical' than the songs themselves. And in a poem about music, this is largely to be achieved through metre.

  There is an exquisite lilt in the first verse. Larkin uses one of the most delicate devices of ten-syllable verse — it is exploited with virtuosity by Dryden and Pope — which is to place the caesura after an unaccented syllable which comes in the middle and not at the end of a foot: such caesuras in iambic verse will be after an odd number of syllables, not an even number.

Examples in the first verse are *lying, circles, mended, coloured, waited*: indeed, they are in every line from line 3 to line 7, and if you break as short a line as line 2, the caesura would be after *covers*. The effect is of lightness of being, a sunny expansiveness which is furthered by the fact that half of the pentameter lines have an extra syllable (lines 4, 5 and 8). But when the songs themselves are 'relearned', there is a change. As if the songs required a stricter beat, there are no extra-metrical syllables in verses two and three. Most of the caesuras occur after an even number of syllables (*tree* in line 13, *time* in 15, *first* in 16, *out* in 18, *incipience, solve, unchangeably, back, hard, then* in 19–24). When the caesuras occur after an odd number of syllables, the effect is rhetorical, as in the postponed caesura before *love* in line 17, or the caesura is deliberately swamped as in line 11. Yet this metrical strictness is paradoxical in that the words which express its message are 'sprawling'. The songs exemplify that fearsome combination which recurs in life in many forms: strict manner and otiose content which, when probed, is delusion. The songs are insistent but not resonant, and the warmth of life is in verse one, in the memories of sun, flowers and children.

Delusion is also Larkin's theme in 'Faith Healing', which was written some three years after 'Love Songs in Age':

Slowly the women file to where he stands
Upright in rimless glasses, silver hair,
Dark suit, white collar. Stewards tirelessly
Persuade them onwards to his voice and hands,
Within whose warm spring rain of loving care
Each dwells some twenty seconds. *Now, dear child,
What's wrong*, the deep American voice demands,
And, scarcely pausing, goes into a prayer
Directing God about this eye, that knee.
Their heads are clasped abruptly; then, exiled

Like losing thoughts, they go in silence; some
Sheepishly stray, not back into their lives
Just yet; but some stay stiff, twitching and loud
With deep hoarse tears, as if a kind of dumb
And idiot child within them still survives

To re-awake at kindness, thinking a voice
At last calls them alone, that hands have come
To lift and lighten; and such joy arrives
Their thick tongues blort, their eyes squeeze grief, a crowd
Of huge unheard answers jam and rejoice —

What's wrong! Moustached in flowered frocks they shake:
By now, all's wrong. In everyone there sleeps
A sense of life lived according to love.
To some it means the difference they could make
By loving others, but across most it sweeps
As all they might have done had they been loved.
That nothing cures. An immense slackening ache,
As when, thawing, the rigid landscape weeps,
Spreads slowly through them — that, and the voice above
Saying *Dear child*, and all time has disproved.

There is much restraint in the first verse, a feeling of satire held
back because Larkin wants to see the healer through the eyes
of the women: criticism is limited to the telling contrast of 'tirelessly' and 'abruptly', the lethally placed 'twenty seconds' and
the ambiguity of 'Directing God' — is God's attention being
drawn to the eye or knees, or is an instruction being issued by
this biblical sounding 'he'? The plight of the women is put in
a wide context. 'In everyone there sleeps/ A sense of life lived
according to love': they are part of us and we of them. Yet if
Larkin's fine statement creates hope for the women — they too
must be capable of love which can 'lift and lighten' — hope is
dispelled by the distinction which follows. Love is about loving
others and selfish love is a contradiction in terms. This is
undeniable in absolute terms; we know it is true: we may like
it not to be true, but we know that the women will not pass this
calmly stated but austere test.

All three poems are about love yet only the later two about
deprivation. 'Wedding-Wind', however, explores an ominously
naïve joy. 'Perpetual' in 'perpetual morning' is a word of time,
the force which has taken its toll in 'Love Songs in Age' and
'Faith Healing'. It is through time that an abiding love is
celebrated. Thus Browning in 'By the Fire-side' reflects on his
years with his wife — both now 'in life's November' — and their
kinship of love with its 'green degrees':

> When, if I think but deep enough,
>> You are wont to answer, prompt as rhyme;
> And you, too, find without rebuff
>> Response your soul seeks many a time
> Piercing its fine flesh-stuff.

But in 'Wedding-Wind' we learn nothing of the character of either partner, and there is no discernible mingling of 'soul piercing its fine flesh-stuff'. Its 'perpetual morning' means physical joy so intense that it feels as if it will be perpetual, and the lady's three questions do not have the strength of enquiries — they are, rather, cries of rapture expressing hopes based on an intensity of pleasure. But their symbol is an unstable one. Gales blow over, wind is changeable. What value in kneeling like cattle outside this fictive world?

Cattle and limits are Larkin's subjects in his early poem 'Wires' (*The Less Deceived*):

> The widest prairies have electric fences,
> For though old cattle know they must not stray
> Young steers are always scenting purer water
> Not here but anywhere. Beyond the wires
>
> Leads them to blunder up against the wires
> Whose muscle-shredding violence gives no quarter.
> Young steers become old cattle from that day,
> Electric limits to their widest senses.

The cattle are a metaphor for humans and, scaled down, the poem is an emblem of one way in which Larkin's imagination works: if a wire is recognised, the 'limit' becomes 'electric' both for its pain and for a release of Larkin's tenderness. In 'Love Songs in Age' the songs promise 'to solve, and satisfy,/ And set unchangeably in order' — their version of 'perpetual morning' — but the pain of recognising their falsehood gives occasion for Larkin to celebrate the lady. She cries, 'lamely admitting how/ It had not done so then, and could not now'. Yet far from 'lamely' being undignified, Larkin invests it with poignancy, even radiance. Her tears are infinitely preferable to the songs' 'glare': they tell of the human lot and our abiding vulnerability. She is alive enough to cry honestly and to admit what hurts.

Not so, alas, the women in 'Faith Healing'. They will not

admit their self-centredness nor see the delusion in their belief that 'a voice/ At last calls them alone'. Their spiritual condition is autistic, 'a kind of dumb/ And idiot child within them still survives'. This is the more sickeningly negative in a poem about faith. The idiot child is a parody of the freshness paradoxically created from experience by the believer: 'Except ye be converted, and become as little children, ye shall not enter into the kingdom of heaven' (Matthew 18 : 3). Yet the power of the poem comes from another dimension. Larkin creates a sense of mental space and the mystery of the mind's workings. It is an interest which appears in his early prose writing and is developed with marvellous brilliance in his poems.

In the climax of his second novel, *A Girl in Winter*, Robin and Jill lie lovelessly in bed together:

> There was the snow, and her watch ticking. So many snow-flakes, so many seconds. As time passed they seemed to mingle in their minds, heaping up into a vast shape that might be a burial mound, or the cliff of an iceberg whose summit is out of sight. Into its shadow dreams crowded, full of conceptions and stirrings of cold, as if iceflows were moving down a lightless channel of water. They were going in orderly slow procession, moving from darkness farther into darkness, allowing no suggestion that their order should be broken, or that one day, however many years distant, the darkness would begin to give place to light.
>
> Yet their passage was not saddening. Unsatisfied dreams rose and fell about them, crying out against their implacability, but in the end glad that such order, such destiny existed. Against this knowledge, the heart, the will, and all that made for protest, could at last sleep.

Here the 'gladness' is in submission and it is as elemental as sleep itself. It is also distanced from the moment of crowding which occurs earlier: 'Into its shadow dreams crowded, full of conceptions and stirrings of cold'. Indeed there is little sense of congestion in the moment of gladness: 'unsatisfied dreams' cry out against the 'implacability', but their motion as they 'rose and fell' is easy, unanguished, almost rhythmical as if they are partly hypnotised by their coming pleasure. The passage owes a debt to Shelley and it has his extraordinary sense of space.

The second verse of 'Faith Healing' (*The Whitsun Weddings*) forms a striking contrast:

> . . . a crowd
> Of huge unheard answers jam and rejoice —

Here congestion and gladness are brought together, and the effect is darkly negative. 'Rejoice' becomes a deliberate puzzle. Is it more than the mere sensation of contact as the answers jam? If this is their only vitality, it seems at best mechanical, and their state before must have been pitiful to the point of terror if release into starved friction gives a sense of life. If an answer is 'unheard', it is impotent, it has lost its nature and any excitement of scale in 'huge' is pointless.

All three poems are about women, 'Wedding-Wind' viewing the intimacy of a marriage night from a female viewpoint. This should alert us to Larkin's liking for distance and its attendant complexities. His striking line, 'What will survive of us is love' might — in isolation — be from the Beatles; in the context of 'An Arundel Tomb' (*The Whitsun Weddings*) it is elaborately modified, though the poet's 'sharp tender shock' gains what is positive from the sculptor's perfunctory motive 'in helping to prolong/ The Latin names around the base'. Larkin occasionally writes of love directly: 'Broadcast' (*The Whitsun Weddings*), for example, enchantingly catches the warmth of his affection and grumpy resentment at a lady's absorption in 'Cascades of monumental slithering'; 'No Road' (*The Less Deceived*), an early work, seems to me one of his finest poems, playing off against each other movements of moody lassitude and energy until the latter is replaced by straining in line 13 to express the dissonant activity of exerting the will for what is negative. Deprivation, however, is his characteristic theme, but what gives stature to his poetry of deprivation is, in part, tenderness and a largeness of mind. At times grumbling, at times harsh, he is also a poet of love.

AFTERTHOUGHTS

1

Explain how Gearin-Tosh makes an analysis of 'Wedding-Wind' central to the argument of this essay.

2

Discuss the importance of imagery drawn from the natural world in the poems cited in this essay.

3

What evidence do you find in Larkin's poetry of 'a largeness of mind' (page 37)?

4

Do you agree that the line, 'What will survive of us is love' might — in isolation — be from the Beatles (page 37)?

John Saunders

*John Saunders is Lecturer in English
Literature at the West Sussex Institute of
Higher Education, and Awarder in
English Literature A-level for the Oxford
and Cambridge Examinations Board.*

ESSAY

Beauty and truth in three poems from *The Whitsun Weddings*

In his short introduction to two poems chosen for an anthology
called *Let the Poet Choose*,[1] Larkin said of his poems that they
might be taken as representative examples of the two kinds of
poetry which he sometimes thought he wrote: 'the beautiful and
the true'. 'Beauty' and 'Truth' have long been considered to be
the proper concern for 'Poetry' and momentarily Larkin's
readers may have seen his statement as an attempt to link his
poetry directly to the great romantic tradition of Wordsworth,
Coleridge, Shelley and Keats. The 'Beauty and Truth' of 'Poetry'
(as contrasted to the ugliness and dishonesty of 'real life') has
been most memorably linked in the lines which end Keats's 'Ode
on a Grecian Urn', a poem which had confidently celebrated the
power of 'Art' — here epitomised in the 'Urn', which Keats
reverently addresses as 'thou' — to transcend time:

---

[1] Ed. James Gibson (London, 1973).

When old age shall this generation waste,
Thou shalt remain, in midst of other woe
Than ours, a friend to man, to whom thou sayst,
'Beauty is truth, truth beauty,' — that is all
Ye know on earth, and all ye need to know.

However, Larkin's introduction went on to mock, rather than to a affirm Keats's famous lines:

> I have always believed that beauty is beauty, truth truth, that is not all ye know on earth nor all ye need to know, and I think a poem usually starts off either from the feeling How beautiful that is or from the feeling How true that is. One of the jobs of the poem is to make the beautiful seem true and the true beautiful, but in fact the disguise can usually be penetrated.

In the essay which follows I shall be looking at three poems from *The Whitsun Weddings* selection: Larkin's two chosen poems standing separately for 'Beauty' ('MCMXIV') and for 'Truth' ('Send No Money'), and the poem which ends the selection, 'An Arundel Tomb', where Larkin attempts to make 'the beautiful seem true and the true beautiful', while leaving a trail of clues to enable the reader to penetrate 'the disguise'.

Beauty in Larkin's poems is most often associated with a past somewhat misremembered — a past which is filtered through nostalgia and made to seem innocent and uncomplicated. Sometimes, as in a poem like 'Love Songs in Age' (*The Whitsun Weddings*), it is 'Love' which is remembered. Often, as in 'Nothing To be Said' (*The Whitsun Weddings*), it is a communal rural past which has subsequently been threatened or destroyed by industrialisation. In 'MCMXIV' Larkin looks back with nostalgia on the beautiful 'innocence' of the mythical England which nearly but never quite existed before the First World War, fought between 1914 and 1918. The poem's title with its roman numerals (MCMXIV, not 1914) succeeds in introducing an initial element of enigma. Many modern readers are likely, at least at first, to 'look, not read'. Perhaps the roman lettering is intended to imbue the England of 1914 with heroic (roman?) values. More obviously, we associate such letterings with inscriptions from the past, especially inscriptions on tombstones, and the poem which follows is an elegaic lament for the England which died in 1914. It is in four stanzas. The first three might be loosely described as a kind of photographic collage, giving a series of predominantly visual impressions of a pre-First World War England. The opening stanza is clearly focused and could well be based on an actual photograph:

> Those long uneven lines
> Standing as patiently
> As if they were stretched outside
> The Oval or Villa Park,
> The crowns of hats, the sun
> On moustached archaic faces
> Grinning as if it were all
> An August Bank Holiday lark

The lines of men are, of course, not queuing for tickets at a cricket or football match. They are waiting to enlist. Soon they will be not spectators but participants in the carnage about to ensue. This is a verbal photograph of men about to die, the 'grinning' (oddly incongruous for 'An August Bank Holiday lark') will soon be the grinning of the dead.

Dead, too, will be the England the men seem here to represent and the two stanzas which follow consist in lists of visual images and associations of an England about to be destroyed by the war and the social changes which followed. It is not a comprehensive nor a logical list — more like a series of predominantly child-like impressions gleaned from old photographs, from films and from children's history books. (Larkin was born in 1922, four years after the war had ended.) Stanza two gives a child's impression of town life rooted in tradition (the 'Established names on the sunblinds'; the 'dark-clothed children at play/ Called after kings and queens'). It is a world made strange by images from the past ('farthings and sovereigns'; 'tin advertisements/ For cocoa and twist'). It is a world perpetually on holiday ('the shut shops'; 'the pubs/ Wide open all day'). Stanza three moves to give a parallel idealised impression of the countryside, free from the order and regimentation, features of the modern world which much distressed Larkin. Here the country is 'not caring'; the 'place-names' are 'all hazed over/ With flowery grasses'. Momentarily, though, just as the 'archaic faces' grin in the opening stanza, there is an intimation of the destruction to come. In an ambiguously evocative image, Larkin remembers the:

> . . . fields
> Shadowing Domesday lines
> Under wheat's restless silence

This image both celebrates the traditional division of the lands of England ('their extent, value, ownership, and liabilities') as recorded in the Domesday book made by order of William the Conqueror in 1086 and, by playing on the non-historical meaning of 'Domesday' as the 'day of judgement', hints at the future where the 'long uneven lines' of the opening stanza will lie, too, 'Under wheat's restless silence'. The stanza then ends with a return to more simple associations of 'differently-dressed servants' living in 'tiny rooms in huge houses' and with a cinematic image of 'The dust behind limousines'. Perhaps these last images are intended to be slightly disturbing to a modern sensibility. Though expressed with a child-like simplicity, they hint at less harmonious and less innocent aspects of Larkin's lost England and suggest less than beautiful 'Truths' about class and power.

However, the final stanza ends any such speculation in its more direct appeal to the reader's emotions. The opening line, 'Never such innocence', crystallises the sense of elegaic nostalgia which has been latent within the images and rhythm of the earlier stanzas. This innocent England was, Larkin wants to believe and wants his readers to believe, about to be lost for ever as it became a part of the past. He appeals directly to our patriotism with an image of the men of England going to war, leaving their gardens and their marriages which could only last 'a little while longer'. The stanza's final line echoes its opening, 'Never such innocence again'.

In marked contrast to the languid, relaxed versification of 'MCMXIV' which helps to lull the reader's mind into accepting as beautiful and true a seductively false and unrepresentative image of reality, the much brisker form of 'Send No Money' — with its tighter rhythm, its insistent alliteration and its brash rhymes — appropriately accompanies a more intellectually difficult poem of ideas. 'Send No Money' is a zany, energetic little poem *about* 'Truth'. It opens with a dialogue between the young poet and 'Time', here personified as a grotesque, over-weight, Victorian gentleman who speaks in a bewildering mixture of cliché ('There's no green in your eye') and bullying directness. The poet, whose contemporaries are keen on experiencing, not questioning, life ('itching to have a bash'), asks Time to reveal to him the truths which underlie experience. Time warns him that the 'truth' about experience will be negative (the kind of vision of existence which lies behind poems as bleak and nihilistic as 'Days' and 'Mr Bleaney' (*The Whitsun Weddings*), perhaps):

> Sit here, and watch the hail
> Of occurrence clobber life out
> To a shape no one sees

The poet gratefully agrees to wait and watch.

The poem's third and final stanza begins with a portrait of the poet in middle age ('Half life is over now'). He gazes 'on dark mornings' into a mirror to see how his own face has been brutally shaped by meaningless experience:

> The bestial visor, bent in
> By the blows of what happened to happen.

And he meditates on the futility of spending a life searching for truth:

> What does it prove? Sod all.
> In this way I spent youth,
> Tracing the trite untransferable
> Truss-advertisement, truth.

These last richly ambiguous lines express the poet's full contempt for having wasted ('spent') the best years of his life in 'tracing' (both following and attempting to copy) 'truth' which he now sees as essentially shallow ('trite') and useless ('untransferable') and which he provocatively likens to a 'Truss-advertisement'. Why a 'Truss-advertisement'? What relationship can there be between 'truth' and an advertisement for a contraption worn to counter the disability caused by a hernia?

In several other poems Larkin uses the idea of the advertisement as an oversimplification of 'Beauty'. In 'Sunny

Prestatyn' (*The Whitsun Weddings*) the 'girl on the poster' attempts to entice the public into believing that a beach holiday with its sun, sand, comfort and easy sex, is a beautiful and easy solution to life. And in 'Essential Beauty' (*The Whitsun Weddings*) a collage of images from advertising seems to offer a seductive haven from the imperfections of real lives dominated by unhappiness and time. In contrast, the 'Truss-advertisement' of 'Send No Money' offers no glamourised picture of existence. It recognises the physical weakness (and, perhaps, sexual impotence) of the potential buyer. The poem's title — 'Send No Money' — is taken directly from the language of mail-order advertisements and suggests that the kind of 'Truth' which Larkin has obtained is essentially cheap, tawdry and clandestine. In this poem there is no attempt to beautify 'Truth'.

In 'An Arundel Tomb' Larkin embarks on a richer, subtler exploration of the interplay between 'Beauty' and 'Truth' and the mediator between them, 'Time'. This is a poem whose central tension results directly from Larkin's emotional need 'to make the beautiful seem true and the true beautiful' and his intellectual refusal to accept this 'untruth'. The beautiful truth which we are half encouraged to accept is encapsulated in the poem's final line:

> What will survive of us is love.

It is tempting to submit to the poem's emotional force and to take this and other lines and half-lines out of context as the 'message' of the poem, while ignoring the trail of evidence which should (perhaps sadly) enable the reader's intellect to counter his or her emotions in order to penetrate 'the disguise'.

'An Arundel Tomb' was occasioned by a visit to Chichester Cathedral which houses the now famous tomb. Larkin was struck by the apparent incongruity between the formal decorum of the medieval monument — with its heraldic outer show and its Latin inscription — and one seemingly modern detail, the holding of hands of the couple in effigy. This incongruity inspired in Larkin a quite remarkable imaginative meditation on the passing of time and the ironic transfiguration which has resulted. The poem is in seven stanzas. A formal description of their structure (each written in six predominantly iambic, four-stress lines, each having the same intricate, *abbcac*, rhyme scheme) might suggest that this is a somewhat rigid, conventional poem. However, within the constraints which he has chosen, Larkin's verse is extraordinarily flexible and succeeds in subtly reinforcing the difference between medieval and modern meaning, a major concern of the poem.

The first two stanzas describe the tomb, placing it clearly within the imagination of the reader, first as a medieval object, then as a modern emblem. Stanza one gives a conventional description of the earl and countess lying together, their faces blurred by time, their dress also blurred but still vaguely providing evidence of their rank and station: he in 'jointed armour', she in 'stiffened pleat'. At their feet — perhaps seen by the modern viewer as a rather embarrassing image of 'fidelity', and so providing 'that faint hint of the absurd' — are 'little dogs'. The poem's form in this opening stanza is made clearly apparent. Each line is end-stopped, giving the stanza something of the 'plain', 'pre-baroque' rigidity of the object described. However, in the second stanza end-stopped lines are abandoned and the reader is made to look beyond the 'plainness of the pre-baroque', seeing through the eyes of the poet. The more flexible verse form here re-enacts Larkin's own experience of discovering the detail which disturbed him. We too notice the earl's 'left-hand gauntlet' clasped empty in the right hand and feel that 'sharp, tender shock' — the 'shock' emphasised by the three strongly stressed syllables which break the iambic pattern — as we experience the suggestion of flesh within the stone:

His hand withdrawn, holding her hand

Stanza three expresses Larkin's musing on the historical significance of the hand-holding, which he suggests was not intended for posterity but was merely a graceful adornment added by the sculptor (for a fee) to please the couple's close friends. The return here to a more formal pattern of line endings assists in giving this stanza a lightness of touch which helps to express the transient sweetness of the gesture. The formality also serves as a foil to the next three stanzas which once again work against the underlying patterning.

Stanzas four, five and six give, with wonderful economy, an imaginative reconstruction of the couple's journey through time ('Their supine stationary voyage'), from the rigid security of the medieval world — a heraldic ('armorial') age in which the 'old tenantry' would 'read' the tomb for its significance within their hierarchical structure — to the 'unarmorial', industrial, modern world in which viewers (like Larkin and the reader) would 'look, not read'. In these three stanzas the passage of time and its destruction of formal decorum is partly communicated through the freedom of the verse, the syntax now recognising neither line nor stanza endings:

> Rigidly they
>
> Persisted, linked, through lengths and breadths
> Of time. Snow fell, undated. Light
> Each summer thronged the glass. A bright
> Litter of birdcalls strewed the same
> Bone-riddled ground. And up the paths
> The endless altered people came,
>
> Washing at their identity.

Within the medieval world the 'identity' of the earl and countess would have seemed eternally secure, their tomb standing as a monument to show that in death they had transcended time. Now, as viewed by the stream of 'altered people' who come to the cathedral, that 'true' identity has been eroded, leaving only 'an attitude' — the couple's significance being confined to the detail of their hand-holding. In the poem's final stanza, Larkin meditates with great eloquence on the meaning of this 'attitude' for the modern viewer.

The diction and rhythm of the final stanza have a heightened intensity. Time has 'transfigured' the earl and countess. Within our world their hand-holding has become 'Their final blazon', an emblem of 'fidelity' which comes near to proving something which Larkin and his readers would very much like to believe:

> and to prove
> Our almost-instinct almost true:
> What will survive of us is love.

The 'prove'/'love' rhyme here may well be intended to echo the concluding couplet of Shakespeare's most confident sonnet on the power of true love to transcend time (number CXVI):

Love's not Time's fool, though rosy lips and cheeks
Within his bending sickle's compass come;
Love alters not with his brief hours and weeks,
But bears it out even to the edge of doom.

If this be error, and upon me proved
I never wrote, nor no man ever loved.

However, although the heightened diction and the energy of the verse in Larkin's final stanza succeed in reinforcing the notion of love as transcendent and triumphant, the actual meaning of the language goes counter to the diction, to the movement of the verse and to the emotion. The earl and countess's attitude may seem 'to prove' something which is 'almost-instinct almost true' but logically something 'almost true' is false. And throughout the poem there have been suggestions that the tomb may not really mean what it seems to mean, that what we would like to take as a beautiful, comforting 'truth' about love, is in fact a deception. The earl and countess 'lie in stone' in more ways than one, and it is — surely — no accident that the word 'lie' is repeated in the opening line of the third stanza: 'They would not think to lie so long', a line which suggests that the 'sculptor's sweet commissioned grace', may itself have been an 'Untruth'.

The tension between 'Beauty' and 'Truth' in 'An Arundel Tomb' is so skilfully articulated that many readers and some commentators have been reluctant to see them as finally irreconcilable. So, for example, George MacBeth in his note on the poem which accompanies his anthology *Poetry 1900 to 1975* (London, 1979) concludes that:

> The simply worded but clearly profoundly felt maxim in the last line 'what will survive of us is love' is built up to and in a way earned by the down-to-earth exactness of the rest of the poem.

In finding the poem 'down-to-earth', MacBeth shows that he has not penetrated Larkin's 'disguise'. Nor has Paul Foster who in an interesting and provocative analysis of the poem concludes that:

The life of the earl and countess that was enshrined in a tomb becomes an artefact to move men centuries later — as, similarly, now, does the artefact that is the poem: not because of their historical witness but through residues of feeling, which seek to prove the permanence of human love.[2]

Both the above commentators completely ignore the opening of the final stanza where Larkin's own words should force the reader to struggle with the 'residues of feeling' to which the poem seems to be appealing:

> Time has transfigured them into
> Untruth.

'Time' in more conventional literary works is an agent of destruction, destroying much that humans value, including 'the innocent and the beautiful'. In 'An Arundel Tomb', as in 'MCMXIV' and other Larkin poems, 'Time' is a creator, not a destroyer, creating our concepts of innocence and beauty. In so doing it works as a grand deceiver which enables us to look at a photograph or an old letter or a baroque detail on a tomb and to murmur — for a moment, but only a moment — 'How beautiful, how true'.

---

[2] See *An Arundel Tomb*, Otter Memorial Paper, no. 1. This pamphlet contains: an analysis of the poem by Paul Foster; a historian's account of the history and symbolism of the tomb by Trevor Brighton; a memoir of Philip Larkin by Patrick Garland; and a set of photographs of the tomb taken by Joy Whiting. The pamphlet is stocked in some bookshops, but is most easily obtained by writing direct to: Dr Paul Foster, Otter Memorial Papers, Bishop Otter College, Chichester, West Sussex PO19 4PE.

AFTERTHOUGHTS

1

'The disguise can usually be penetrated' (page 40). How important is the penetrating of disguise in Larkin's poetry?

2

Compare Saunders's interpretation of 'MCMXIV' (pages 40–42) with Gardiner's (page 68). What differences emerge?

3

What significance does Saunders attach to Larkin's choice of the word 'lie' in 'An Arundel Tomb' (page 47)?

4

Do you agree with Saunders's argument that, in Larkin's poetry, '"Time" is a creator, not a destroyer' (page 48)?

Peter Hollindale

*Peter Hollindale is Senior Lecturer in
English and Education at the University
of York, and has published numerous
critical books and articles.*

ESSAY

The long perspectives

> Truly, though our element is time,
> We are not suited to the long perspectives
> Open at each instant of our lives.
>
> ('Reference Back', *The Whitsun Weddings*)

A conspicuous recurrent feature of Philip Larkin's poetry is his
preoccupation with two kinds of 'long perspective'. The first is
a vision of the individual life and its shape, viewed from some
point in middle age from which the mind can look back in retrospect on youth, with its characteristic feelings and hopes, and
can also look forward in knowledgeable, disturbed anticipation
to the future and the approach of old age and death. The second
perspective is the similar but larger and more scaring one, of
the living being confronted by the knowledge of inevitable
death, and setting *all* life, all experience, against an imaginative
vision of dying and death as experiences in themselves. In this
essay I shall try to illustrate the importance for Larkin of these
two perspectives, and suggest that his most typical stance
towards life-experience is that of the informed and unillusioned
observer or spectator, while towards death-experience his typical
stance is that of a deeply troubled sharer in the fate which is
common to all people and yet always lonely and particular.

Again and again Larkin's poems open out into realisation

of these saddening or frightening perspectives, abolishing any sense of firmness or trust in the present moment by revealing it to be surrounded by illusion, instability or vacancy. Yet there is one part of life where the relentless logic of Larkin's imagination is suspect, and produces inconsistencies and contradictions between one poem and another, or even within a single poem. It comes when he looks at the 'instant of our lives' when the 'long perspectives' are *not* open, because life has so far been too brief to disclose them or to make them urgent: the 'instant' of childhood, youth and early adult life, before a middle age of the imagination has set in.

The poem 'I Remember, I Remember' (*The Less Deceived*) is one of Larkin's best-known, but it is not necessarily a very helpful guide either to the understanding of his work in general, or to his truest feelings about early life. The perspective, characteristically, is that of the middle-aged man looking back on the past, and the stance is that of the spectator, glancing out at the home town of his childhood from a passing train. Its subject is typical of Larkin: emptiness, non-occurrence, not-being. It describes a childhood which didn't happen. In spite of the famous, aphoristic closing line, 'Nothing, like something, happens anywhere,' with its tone of wry, accepting resignation, the dominant impression left by the poem is one of subdued resentment, as if the very lack of significant memories were itself a pointer to childhood unhappiness. This effect is produced by a serious misjudgement of tone on Larkin's part, in the lines:

> 'You look as if you wished the place in Hell,'
> My friend said, 'judging from your face.'

The friend's remark is emotively strong, and also dramatically strong, offering as it does a sudden indication of how the poet-observer is himself observed. But its sentiment is far too negative to fit the mood or content of the poem hitherto. Before these closing, alienated lines, the poem has been an amused satire on the most hackneyed incidents of novels and autobiographies about early life. It has been a *literary* poem, about a literary man's denial of a literary childhood, not a denunciation of the real thing. The last lines convert it into something more serious and discordant. Two kinds of retrospect are grating against each other.

Larkin does the same thing, more briefly and generally, in the poem 'Coming' (*The Less Deceived*), an attractive lyric celebrating the imminence of spring:

> And I, whose childhood
> Is a forgotten boredom,
> Feel like a child
> Who comes on a scene
> Of adult reconciling,
> And can understand nothing
> But the unusual laughter,
> And starts to be happy.

Like the last line of 'I Remember, I Remember', the expression 'a forgotten boredom' has become well known, and is often quoted out of context. Within its context in this poem, there is something extraneous and intrusive about the phrase. The remaining six lines are a most precise and delicate registration of childhood feeling, rendered with a wholly convincing simplicity. No one whose childhood was entirely a forgotten boredom could remember this psychological experience so well, or fabricate it so authentically. It is an experienced truth. Again we have a dissonance of feeling, experience jarring against attitude. It is a repeated and typical habit of Larkin not to let any expressions of imaginative delight slip past the censoring intelligence without some cautionary reservation. He is determined not to be tricked or deceived into slack admissions of unwarranted happiness. The spectator in Larkin — self-personified as middle-aged, judgemental and knowing — is sometimes unduly watchful for unjustified ventures into direct and spontaneous experience, especially if the experience is happy.

Larkin's professions of childhood as an unremembered blankness (which surface again in the poem 'Forget What Did', *High Windows*) are contradicted by the prose commentary he wrote on 'I Remember, I Remember' called 'Not the Place's Fault', first published in the Coventry arts magazine *Umbrella* (I.iii, summer 1959) and recently reprinted in the memorial volume *An Enormous Yes*, edited by Harry Chambers (Peterloo Poets, 1986). This delightful piece is full of vivid childhood memories. Larkin's early life, may have been fairly ordinary and uneventful, but it was not by his own account lonely or unhappy, nor yet boring, and it is certainly not forgotten. There is amusement and affection in the detailed recall:

> I sometimes think the slight scholarly stoop in my bearing today was acquired by looking for cigarette cards in Coventry gutters. There seemed to be a 'Famous Cricketers' series every summer then . . .
>
> ('Not the Place's Fault')

and it reappears, still coloured by enjoyment and affection, in the poem 'To the Sea' (*High Windows*), where the family seaside holiday is celebrated:

> As half an annual pleasure, half a rite,
>
> As when, happy at being on my own,
> I searched the sand for Famous Cricketers

Clearly there is ambivalence in Larkin's recollection of his childhood, or in his mature attitude to it. It is formally dismissed as a blanked-out, unremembered time, and as such it obeys the consistent ordinance of Larkin's world whereby time remorselessly passes without being significantly used. That is to say, early life is caused to conform to the pessimistic pattern which Larkin, courageously deceptionless, discovers in the whole of existence. Offset against this formal blankness is a quite different attitude towards childhood and youthfulness, one of affection, and loss, and pained envy of those who briefly enjoy it now.

There is a paradox in this which is central to Larkin's conception of time. It is the compulsory inconsistency, so to speak, in his otherwise bleakly consistent awareness of what constitutes a *lifetime*. All lives are death-bound, and throughout their length are undercut by that appalling fact. All lives, moreover, are progressively damaged by the constraints of choices, irrevocable once made, and by failures, disappointments and missed opportunities. Even youth, from the detached overview which sees its place in lifetime as a whole, is bound by the same negative law as maturity and old age. But in so far as maturity and pessimistic awareness are things we travel to, in so far as Larkin's pessimistic truths are *discovered* truths, then youth is set apart from the rest, a time of innocence and possibility which precedes the disenchanted knowingness of middle life. It is therefore to be envied by the time-haunted poet, however conscious he is of its fragility.

Consequently Larkin the spectator is repeatedly preoccupied with beginnings, both in human and in natural life. Rather than the closing dismissiveness of 'I Remember, I Remember', the more customary tone is one of affection and pleasure, even if they are usually linked to a sense of time and loss. Larkin is not usually thought of as a nature poet, but his slender output includes at least four evocations of spring ('Coming' and 'Spring', *The Less Deceived*; 'First Sight', *The Whitsun Weddings* and 'The Trees', *High Windows*) and the beautiful lyric 'Cut Grass' (*High Windows*) is a fifth, if we accept as we should its tender insistence on brevity and death. These poems have human equivalents. 'Born Yesterday' (*The Less Deceived*) is a poem for a newly born infant which, for all the scrupulous, non-committal, Larkinesque caution which encloses it, is still a kind of blessing and a guarded prediction of possible happiness. In several other poems ('Lines on a Young Lady's Photograph Album' and 'Maiden Name', *The Less Deceived*; 'How Distant', *High Windows*) the youth which is accorded such admiration, affection and value is already over, already out of reach in the personal or historical past. It is as if Larkin can only truly release his sensuous delight in youth once its conditional nature and obedience to the laws of time have been built into the poem's form. Usually, too, there must be some declaration of the poet's own superannuated exile from the times and beings he is praising. In these habitual cautionary ways the intellect (which acts as spectator) is pacified and allows the imagination to run free.

The poem in which this is most explicitly clear is 'Sad Steps' (*High Windows*). Larkin's self-characterisation at the start of the poem is undignified and self-reductive ('Groping back to bed after a piss.'). Thus guarded from any possible charge of romantic self-idealising, the poet looks out through the curtains at a townscape in moonlight, and the special clarity of the night scene brings associations with it. The moonlight scene:

> Is a reminder of the strength and pain
> Of being young; that it can't come again,
> But is for others undiminished somewhere.

Like the poet's own time-bound separateness, the element of time itself and necessary change is declared in these lines, but within that shell of truthfulness is something softer, more affirmative, more vulnerable: an expression of *value* in the transient intensity of youthfulness, and a feeling of deep loss that it is personally over (the verb 'can't' suggests a deprivation and saddened longing which would not have been conveyed by the truthfully impersonal 'won't'). The last line is unmistakably envious.

Moreover, this closing line includes the imprecise but crucial word 'somewhere', as if the lost experience cannot be exactly and conveniently allocated to a 'stage of life' called youth, but belongs instead to some impossibly distant place which lies far beyond reach or definition. Expressions of indefinite time and place are always important signals in Larkin's poetry. So are vocabulary and images of endlessness and vacancy. Because the essential words are often commonplace and unspecific (for example 'somewhere', 'anywhere', 'always') it is easy to overlook them. In truth they are central to Larkin's way of describing human desolation.

'Sad Steps' is a powerful and highly characteristic poem. It starts with a brutally realistic self-characterisation, then puts the characterised poet in the situation of a middle-aged spectator, and finally enlarges his solitary vision by placing it forlornly amid expanding metaphysical distances. It is a 'long perspective' indeed. Notice the paradoxical situation of youth itself in this vision. It is part of the pattern (because the same fate will overtake it in due time) but also enviably separate from it (because youth does not know its fate and is briefly protected by the innocent intensity of youth itself).

Springtime, then, can be a redeeming positive, both literal and metaphorical, in Larkin's generally astringent and despairing view of human life. However, the chosen persona of Larkin's poetry has always passed this stage; his implied speaker is invariably middle-aged. Usually he is a passive figure, disqualified by the penalty of insight from naïve participation in the futile activity of life. He can take delight in the human spectacle, especially of ritualistic pleasure, but his role (as in the celebrating poem 'Show Saturday', *High Windows*) is usually that of the observer and reporter.

The passive nature of the present is inescapable once the

vision afforded by the 'long perspective' has opened up. In Larkin's imaginative vision the present moment is a trap. The trap is set by the past and the future, two cruel gamekeepers at work on human life. Because of its unblinking clarity, the poem 'Triple Time' (*The Less Deceived*) is a key to much of Larkin's other writing; the cool logic of its spare three-stanza structure defines the trap precisely. The present, which is empty and neuter ('A time unrecommended by event') is simultaneously the time to which we looked forward in earlier years as the richly productive future, and also simultaneously the past we shall look back on in the years ahead, as a place of missed opportunities. Thus, in 'Triple Time', the present is always (once the 'long perspectives' have opened) an emptiness populated by the ghostly hopes of our past and the ghostly disappointments of our future, but it is also a time which grows steadily more impoverished, so it is on this trap that finally:

> we blame our last
> Threadbare perspectives, seasonal decrease.

The disturbing paradox of this poem's closing lines is essentially the same pessimistic one that I have suggested can be found in the poems of youth and spring: life is always the same terminal condition, but it also gets worse.

We should be quite wrong, however, to view Larkin's poems as simply variations on his own bleak judgement. He is a more diverse poet than some critics suggest, and often surprises us. I have already pointed to the lyrical and joyous affirmations which exist (no matter how much screened by self-exclusion or reminders about time) in the poems of youth and spring. The variety of his work is due to the varying transactions between the poet's intellect and his imagination. Larkin himself distinguished clearly and significantly between these two terms. In an early essay contributed to a magazine symposium on 'The Writer in his Age', he suggested that the two qualities may well be at odds with each other. He criticised:

> a concept of good writing far too dependent on the intellect and the social conscience to be acceptable, for the imagination is not the servant of these things, and may even be at variance with them

> (*London Magazine*, vol. 4, no. 5, May 1957)

and he stressed that a precondition of good writing is that it originates in and excites the imagination. In the same essay he said something which is ostensibly about the reader, but in fact is full of implications for the understanding of his own work and its composition:

> A writer must have regard for the negative truthfulness necessary to sneak his poem or story past the reader's logical threshold.

This is a very important statement indeed. Larkin is effectively saying that certain things must be intellectually admitted within a piece of writing before the reader can accept its authority as a work of imagination. I would argue that this is precisely what he does *to himself*, in the process of composition. In many of his poems one can see Larkin carefully satisfying the intellectual preconditions for imaginative release. Larkin's great enemy is self-deception; his intellectual and artistic fears are self-indulgence and spurious comfort . His work has to satisfy his own statement, 'Poetry is an affair of sanity, of seeing things as they are.'[1] Once the rigorous, censoring intellect has been appeased, the imagination is free to travel in the open air and go where it wishes. Undeniably the results can be — more often than not — alarming and frightening, as the imagination escapes into spatial and temporal dimensions of a disturbing kind. 'Sad Steps' is an example of this. So is 'Next, Please' (*The Less Deceived*), in which a neat metaphor of ships and sailing is transformed in the final stanza into a nightmarish symbol of a death-ship voyaging on seas of nothingness.

Not all the outcomes are pessimistic, however. A small but important minority of Larkin's poems present a different kind of transcendent imaginative vision. The finest of these is 'The Whitsun Weddings', and it can be revealing to examine this poem's gradual approach to its marvellous, transfiguring final stanza. It begins, typically, with self-characterisation: the poet is the obscure solitary traveller, detachedly aware of the passing sunlit landscape. Once the platform scenes attract his attention, he becomes more fully the spectator, observing and reporting in

---

[1] '"Big Victims": Emily Dickinson and Walter de la Mare', *Required Writing*, p. 197

vivid, graphic detail the appearance of the wedding-parties. Gradually, in the fifth stanza (preceded in the fourth by one tiny anticipatory detail, 'An uncle shouting smut') description of appearance gives way to inferences about the feelings and attitudes held by those left behind towards the newly married couples who are now aboard the train.

The crucial, pivotal lines in the poem come as the platform parties are finally left behind:

> Free at last,
> And loaded with the sum of all they saw,
> We hurried towards London . . .

(The Whitsun Weddings)

The 'we' is significant. The couples are 'free' (on their own together and released, after the crowded social event of marriage) but so is the poet and the poet's imagination. He has become something more than observer. He is an accidental *sharer* in the event through sharing the couples' honeymoon journey, just as they accidentally share each other's. What he sees through the window ('someone running up to bowl') is now what they see. For each couple, 'their lives would all contain this hour', and Larkin's life contains it also. Two things have happened. The spectator has become the co-participant, and the hour of the shared journey has become a uniquely extended moment, a single time-frame, redeemed for once from the present's emptiness by the unquestionable significance of the life-experience it contains.

So, 'free at last', the imagination can reach the optimistic, regenerative vision of the closing stanza. Earlier — starting off with the smut-shouting uncle — Larkin has hinted at the varied, half-conscious sexual excitement of those left behind. For the men it is broadly comic, a farcical success; for the women it is 'a happy funeral' or 'a religious wounding'. There is something vicariously aroused and active in the happiness of those left on the platforms, dispatching couples into an unknown future of sexual life and potential new birth. Something of that festive tension, something of the couples' own resolve, something of the poet's complicity in it, are bound together in the complex half-line 'There we were *aimed*'. The word 'aimed' then releases the rich closing image of the arrow-shower and the rain, the happy aggression of this ceremonial shot into the future ('arrow-shower') merging imperceptibly with the fertility and procreativeness of 'rain'. It is a happy vision for the spectator-poet, but we should still notice that this liberating event is '*somewhere* becoming rain'. 'Somewhere' is not so desolate a word here as it is in 'Sad Steps', but its spatial vagueness still has the power to exclude: neither the poet nor the wedding-crowds have a place in the ultimate fulfilment.

Despite these exceptions, however, Larkin's poetry is dominated by the longest perspective of all: death. And in this event he is not the spectator, not the accidental sharer, but a helpless co-participant in the universal private fate. His bleakest, most uncompromising expression of it comes in the late poem, 'Aubade':[2]

> . . . I see what's really always there:
> Unresting death, a whole day nearer now,
> Making all thought impossible but how
> And where and when I shall myself die.
> Arid interrogation: yet the dread
> Of dying, and being dead,
> Flashes afresh to hold and horrify.

In an interview Larkin once remarked, 'I can only say I dread endless extinction.' The remark is very precise, and all I wish to do here is to stress these two dominant aspects of Larkin's fear of death: extinction and endlessness. This is the nature of his 'long perspective': the human journey from being to not-being, from time to timelessness, from place to vacancy. In the second stanza of 'Aubade', he specifies his dread in just this way:

> . . . the total emptiness for ever,
> The sure extinction that we travel to
> And shall be lost in always. Not to be here,
> Not to be anywhere,
> And soon; nothing more terrible, nothing more true.

Death for Larkin is dissolution, oblivion and emptiness. The long perspective of death both enhances the value of precarious

---

[2] First published in *The Times Literary Supplement*, 23 December 1977.

life and fatally undermines the possible significance of all that life can offer. To contemplate death in this way is disabling: it transforms life into something that can only be held too consciously, at the cost of our power to live it, and yet it makes life itself an object of multifarious and painful wonder. This feeling is expressed in 'The Old Fools' (*High Windows*), where the vacuum that preceded birth is compared with the vacuum ahead of us:

> At death, you break up: the bits that were you
> Start speeding away from each other for ever
> With no one to see. It's only oblivion, true:
> We had it before, but then it was going to end,
> And was all the time merging with a unique endeavour
> To bring to bloom the million-petalled flower
> Of being here. Next time you can't pretend
> There'll be anything else.

When he observes the process of dying, as in 'Ambulances' (*The Whitsun Weddings*) or 'The Building' (*High Windows*), Larkin is the involved spectator, the participant-to-be, aware of his future enforced conscription in the shared fate. This fate is declared in uncompromising, self-threatening phrases: 'Well,/ We shall find out' in 'The Old Fools', or 'All streets in time are visited', in 'Ambulances' (*The Whitsun Weddings*). But beyond the clinical truth of dying lie the metaphysical truths of death, and it is here that Larkin's perspective is uniquely his own and uniquely terrifying. Larkin's imaginative vision of death is a kind of agoraphobia. It is a dread of open spaces: the greatest open spaces of all, those of infinity and eternity. It is a fear of the extinction and obliteration of the self in the face of nightmare vastness. This is the 'solving emptiness/ That lies just under all we do' ('Aubade'): an emptiness that *dissolves*, not one that provides solutions. Surrounded by the emptiness, life is a closed, well-lit and furnished room from which we may at any moment be evicted. Only in a few poems does the void lie open, but when it does, as in the poems I have mentioned — and perhaps most powerfully of all in the closing stanzas of 'Next, Please' (*The Less Deceived*) and 'High Windows' — it discloses a vision of death which is as far-reaching and disturbing as any in the language.

AFTERTHOUGHTS

1

What two 'perspectives' are identified by Hollindale at the beginning of this essay?

2

'Expressions of indefinite time and place are always important signals in Larkin's poetry' (page 55). Do you agree? And signals of *what*?

3

'Beyond the clinical truth of dying lie the metaphysical truths of death' (page 60). What distinction is being drawn here?

4

Compare this essay with the essays by Day on pages 81–92 and by Draper on pages 95–104. What similarities and differences do you find?

Alan Gardiner

*Alan Gardiner is a Lecturer in English
Language and Literature at Redbridge
Technical College, and is the author of
numerous critical studies.*

ESSAY

Larkin's England

When the narrator of 'Dockery and Son' (*The Whitsun
Weddings*) changes trains at Sheffield and eats while he is
waiting an 'awful pie', Philip Larkin strikes a chord of sympathetic response in every English reader. His poems are full of such
detail, evoking an England that is immediately recognisable.
The landscape of his poetry, a mixture of the urban and the
rural, is one that we have all observed: wheat-fields, city centres
thronged with shoppers, canals, hedges, cooling towers. Moreover, the narrative voice in most of Larkin's poems belongs to
somebody who has experiences with which the reader can
readily identify and whose attitudes we can easily share. From
these poems there emerges a consistent picture of an ordinary,
unpretentious man: a bicycle-clipped lover of unspoilt English
countryside and pre-Charlie Parker jazz, who resents the
mundane routine of work but would feel lost without it, whose
unglamorous childhood is a 'forgotten boredom', who is dissat-
isfied with the present but fearful of the future. Larkin's ability
to capture with such accuracy the quality of life as it is actually
lived in contemporary England accounts for much of his popu-
larity, but his achievement as a poet clearly amounts to more
than this: his poems may be rooted in a familiar social reality
but they also transcend this reality and have the universality
and the timelessness that we associate with great poetry.

'Here', the opening poem of *The Whitsun Weddings*, is representative of Larkin's strengths. In the first three stanzas the journey to Hull, and the city itself, are presented in graphic detail. The surging momentum of the poem's opening lines imitates the 'swerving' motion of the train, and the dense, cluttered description effectively suggests a landscape observed at speed: industry gives way to fields and farms, then the train travels alongside a widening estuary before Hull is finally reached. In describing the city Larkin vividly re-creates the appearance and atmosphere of a busy, crowded port: the cranes, tattoo-shops and consulates, the 'grain-scattered streets' and 'grim head-scarfed wives'. The random acquisitiveness of the shoppers who converge on the town's department stores, however, makes them indistinguishable from the crowds to be found in any other urban centre. But Larkin's journey does not end here (though that of the train, presumably, does). He takes us past the city's expanding suburban sprawl to an area of quiet, isolated villages. There is activity here also, but of a very different kind; in these surroundings can be sensed the hidden life of nature, as 'leaves unnoticed thicken' and 'neglected waters quicken'. The final lines take us further still, to a beach and the sea beyond it, and the poem ends with a vision of an unattainable peace, free from the congestion and the pressures of urban living. The poem has thus been more than a description of an actual train journey to the north-east of England, excellent though that description is. The quietness and solitude beyond the city bring the poet closer to the vital forces of life, and encourage a longing for a spiritual as well as a physical escape from human society.

The movement in 'Here' from the precise, detailed observation of the opening three stanzas to the broader perspective of the poem's conclusion is characteristic of Larkin's poetry. His poems frequently have a specific, localised context but this does not inhibit the expression of a more generalised vision of human experience. Also characteristic is Larkin's role as a detached observer who is in society but at the same time distanced from it. It is significant that Larkin should have chosen to live in Hull for most of his adult life. In a 1964 television interview with Sir John Betjeman he said that Hull appealed to him because he liked living 'on the edge of things'. He responded to the atmosphere of a busy, working city but Hull's remoteness from the rest of England also attracted him. His Foreword to *A Rumoured City* (Bloodaxe Books, Newcastle-on-Tyne, 1983) described Hull as 'a city that is in the world, yet sufficiently on the edge of it to have a different resonance ... its face half-turned towards distance and silence, and what lies beyond them'.

'The Whitsun Weddings' (*The Whitsun Weddings*) describes another train journey, though this time in the opposite direction — from Hull to London. Larkin is again the detached observer, both of the towns and countryside which flash past the speeding train, and of the wedding-parties gathered on the railway station platforms at each stop. In the first two stanzas the emphasis is on the former, and as in 'Here' we see Larkin's skill at evoking the physical reality of the English landscape. It is a landscape in which the industrial alternates with the agricultural: farms and cattle are succeeded first by polluted canals and then by hedges and grass, before breakers' yards full of dismantled cars signal the approach of another town. In the middle stanzas of the poem it is Larkin's mastery of social observation that is demonstrated as he describes in precise, unflattering detail the groups of wedding guests that have come from receptions in 'banquet-halls up yards' to see off the newly married couples: he notes their rowdiness and vulgarity ('mothers loud and fat;/ An uncle shouting smut') and their synthetic elegance ('the perms,/ The nylon gloves and jewellery substitutes'). The amused, somewhat disdainful tone underlines Larkin's detachment, but as the poem moves towards its conclusion in the final two stanzas he reflects on the deeper meaning of what he has seen and asserts, albeit tentatively, that it is something of positive human value. The train approaches London (the careful selection of detail again evoking a realistic landscape — an Odeon, a cooling tower, a cricketer running up to bowl) and Larkin ponders the 'frail/ Travelling coincidence' that has brought these couples together. He compares London's postal districts to packed 'squares of wheat' and the married couples about to alight from the train to 'an arrow- shower/ Sent out of sight, somewhere becoming rain'. The latter image is appropriate partly because after travelling together on the train the passengers will go their separate ways and be dispersed over

London, but it also suggests that the married couples are at the beginning of a new life, one that Larkin associates with fertility and growth: they will be as rain falling on fields of wheat.

'The Whitsun Weddings' observes, and ultimately celebrates, an English social ritual. Other poems express a similar approbation for some of society's other habits and customs. One such is 'Show Saturday' (*High Windows*), which describes a country show in abundant and affectionate detail. The poem traces the course of the day, from the beginning of the show when cars jam the surrounding country lanes to the end when lorries are loaded and the car park empties. As well as this chronological progression we have the impression of a leisurely tour of the show, Larkin moving steadily around the enclosures and tents. The profusion of human interests, activities and skills represented at the show clearly impresses him. The home-grown vegetables are set out in rows 'Of single supreme versions', the eggs and scones are 'pure excellences'. Other events include wrestling, showjumping and a chainsaw competition. The spectators and participants are observed with gently ironic amusement: competing wives 'glaring' at each other's jellies, husbands 'on leave from the garden'. As the crowds depart Larkin thinks of the homes they are returning to (in 'one-street villages' and the side roads of small towns) and of the lives they lead during the rest of the year (running small businesses, drinking in public houses on market days). Here, as throughout the poem, we are struck by the 'Englishness' of what is described: newspapers sticking out of letterboxes, allotments beside railway lines. After this prolonged accumulation of detail Larkin's profoundest insights emerge (as in 'Here' and 'The Whitsun Weddings') at the close of the poem. Rituals such as the country show are of value partly because they *are* rituals, traditions which preserve society's links with its past, and partly because of their communal nature: the show is something for people to 'share', an annual renewal of human kinship that 'breaks ancestrally each year into/ Regenerate union'. The poem ends on a note of emphatic affirmation: 'Let it always be there'.

'To the Sea' (*High Windows*) is another poem which observes the English at leisure. The poet watches families on

C

their annual seaside holiday and recalls the family holidays of his own childhood. The scene is rendered with Larkin's customary exactness: the faint sound of transistor radios, a distant ship on the horizon, cigars and chocolate-papers littering the beach. As an adult, the poet feels alienated from the activity around him ('Strange to it now . . .') but he derives comfort and reassurance from the knowledge that the English seaside holiday is a tradition ('half an annual pleasure, half a rite') that is 'Still going on'. It fosters a simple, undemonstrative consideration for others: nervous children are helped to overcome their fear of the sea and the old in their wheelchairs are given the opportunity to enjoy a 'final summer'.

In both 'Show Saturday' and 'To the Sea' (*High Windows*) there is the implication that social rituals are also important as a means of resisting or defying the passage of time; their regularity enables us to have some sense of human permanence. In 'Show Saturday' the crowds at the show are oblivious of 'time's rolling smithy-smoke', and in 'To the Sea' Larkin recalls how as a child on the beach he felt that time was standing still: the white steamer on the horizon appeared motionless, 'stuck in the afternoon'. In 'Toads Revisited' (*The Whitsun Weddings*) it is the ritual of work rather than leisure which is a source of strength. The prospect of a life of idleness, spent aimlessly wandering around the local park, at first entices the poet, but he is then deterred by the emptiness of such an existence. With nothing to occupy one's thoughts, one would be left to observe the relentless passing of time. Work may be tedious and repetitive but it gives our lives shape, order and meaning (however illusory) and so wards off thoughts of eventual death.

'Church Going' (*The Less Deceived*) is, as its cleverly ambiguous title suggests, about a ritual that has fallen into decline. A visit to an empty church causes the narrator to wonder what will become of churches when they have fallen completely out of use. The poem begins as an account of a personal experience but in the third stanza 'I' changes to 'we' and Larkin addresses broader issues: what the Church has meant to our society, and the meaning it now has in an increasingly secular age. Even in the early stanzas, however, Larkin's depiction of himself encourages us to see him as a representative figure — an ordinary, faithless Englishman. He enters the church cautiously, after checking to make sure that nothing is going on inside, and then glances cursorily around him. His description of the interior has an air of boredom and indifference, as well as revealing his limited knowledge of churches. There is 'some brass and stuff/ Up at the holy end' and he cannot tell whether the roof has been cleaned or restored. Nevertheless, in a clumsily reverential gesture he removes his bicycle clips. Eventually he prepares to leave, reflecting that the church was not worth stopping for. But wondering why he *did* stop leads the poet to discover in himself 'A hunger . . . to be more serious', which the church does something to satisfy and which, he believes, mankind will always possess. Churches for generations have dealt within their walls with the important experiences of life — birth, marriage and death — and encouraged us to think of these events with an appropriate gravity. When they crumble into ruins society will be diminished by their loss, although the human needs and impulses that the Church represents will survive.

In his later poems Larkin increasingly concerned himself with overtly 'public' themes and pondered, as he had in 'Church Going', on society's future. Frequently these poems record with dismay the steady erosion of the England of the past and foresee its eventual destruction. 'Going, Going' (*High Windows*), a poem commissioned by the Department of the Environment, deplores the obliteration of the rural landscape. In the poem Larkin says he had once felt that there would always be fields and farms 'beyond the town', that although waste was thrown into the sea 'The tides will be clean beyond' (the vision of a purer environment 'beyond' is reminiscent of 'Here'), but the speed of the urban and industrial advance now unnerves him: 'For the first time I feel somehow/ That it isn't going to last.' Fed by the financial greed of developers and industrialists and the greed of the young for yet more houses and parking spaces, the process will soon be complete:

> And that will be England gone,
> The shadows, the meadows, the lanes,
> The guildhalls, the carved choirs.

The ironically titled 'Homage to a Government' (*High Windows*) is Larkin's most explicitly political poem. The withdrawal of British troops from abroad in order to save money (the poem was written in 1969) seemed to Larkin a national humiliation. As he later explained, it was the fact that the government's decision was made purely on the grounds of financial expediency that appalled him. Future generations, the poem suggests, will be living in a country where honour, duty and responsibility no longer matter. Statues of military heroes and national leaders will remain as reminders of our imperial past, but the England that built them will no longer exist.

If contemporary life fills Larkin with despondency and trepidation, he recalls England's past with a corresponding wistfulness and nostalgia. 'MCMXIV' (*The Whitsun Weddings*) is an idealised portrait of England before the outbreak of the First World War. There is the familiar accumulation of impressionistic detail, but used here to evoke a vanished way of life: moustached men in hats, sombrely dressed children named after kings and queens, farthings and sovereigns, tin advertisements for cocoa and tobacco. The poem is written as a single sentence and has no main verb, the effect of which is to suggest a settled, unchanging calm. The life that is depicted is one rooted deep in the past: the plots of farmland stretch back to the Domesday Book, the blinds on the shop-fronts bear the names of long 'established' traders, and the men's faces appear 'archaic'. But this continuity with the past was about to end. When Larkin states that there was 'Never such innocence again', he does not only mean that the 'grinning' men queuing to enlist were unprepared for the horrors of the trenches. He is alluding also to the social and industrial developments of the twentieth century that would fundamentally change English life. Habits, customs and traditions that were still a part of our national culture in 1914 (the year is made to appear even more remotely distant by the use of roman numerals) are now irretrievably lost to us.

In several of Larkin's poems the shortcomings of contemporary human society are offset by the strength and beauty of the natural world, which is seen as a source of consolation, even though (as 'Going, Going' illustrates) that world is felt to be increasingly under threat. In 'Coming' (*The Less Deceived*) the poet is cheered by the birdsong and the brightening evenings that announce the arrival of spring. His happiness is compared to that of a child who, witnessing a scene of adult reconciliation, does not understand what is taking place but responds to the sound of laughter. The comparison suggests several things: that nature has a mysterious, hidden life, that the world does not always appear so harmonious a place, and that the narrator's pleasure is an instinctive, unthinking reaction. In 'The Trees' (*High Windows*) spring is given a more qualified welcome. The new leaves that appear annually on the trees may suggest an endless process of rejuvenation, in contrast to the ageing experienced by human beings. But, Larkin observes, the rings inside the trunk of each tree record the passing of time and eventually the trees, like ourselves, will die. Nevertheless, despite their mortality, the burgeoning trees are an encouragement to human endeavour, urging the poet to 'Begin afresh, afresh, afresh'.

'At Grass' (*The Less Deceived*) presents an idyllic and distinctively English rural scene. Two racehorses have retired from a hectic life of 'Cups and Stakes and Handicaps' and are free to enjoy the tranquillity of the countryside. They have retreated into anonymity: they are no longer identified by name and when they are first sighted 'The eye can hardly pick them out'. The poet, it is implied, yearns for a similar anonymity — we are again reminded of the wish to withdraw from society in 'Here' — but the peace he desires is unattainable.

The 'Englishness' of Larkin's poetry has led to accusations of insularity. He certainly appears to have had little interest in other cultures and societies; asked by an interviewer if he would like to travel abroad he admitted he was 'singularly incurious about other places'. His poems have been shown to owe a certain amount to the French symbolists of the nineteenth century, but Larkin preferred to ally himself with an English poetic tradition whose members include Hardy (frequently acknowledged as his major influence), Wilfred Owen and William Barnes. Amongst his contemporaries he admired Betjeman and the novelist Barbara Pym, both writers whose work, like Larkin's, faithfully depicted English life as they knew or remembered it. Larkin's poems are recognisably of our time, and our society, but is this necessarily a weakness? He once said that he wondered if it ever occurred to critics who accused him of writing 'a kind of Welfare State sub-poetry' that he actually agreed with them. He went on to say that he wrote the kind of poetry he had to write, and that such poetry was inevitably influenced by the environment in which he lived. The alleged 'provincialism' of Larkin's poetry is actually one of its greatest strengths. He does not evade the larger human issues — love, transience, death — but places them in a context which gives his treatment of them a remarkable and wholly convincing reality.

AFTERTHOUGHTS

1

How accessible would Larkin's poetry be to a *non*-English reader?

2

What importance does Gardiner suggest for Larkin's focus on 'ritual' (pages 65–66)?

3

Compare Gardiner's interpretation of 'MCMXIV' (page 68) with Saunders's (pages 40–42). What differences emerge?

4

What do you understand by 'provincialism' (page 70)? What arguments does Gardiner put forward in this essay to defend Larkin against such a charge?

Harvey Hallsmith

Harvey Hallsmith is Head of English at Charterhouse School, and Awarder in English Literature A-level for the Oxford and Cambridge Examinations Board.

ESSAY

The 'I' in Larkin

Philip Larkin once said of himself in one of his rare newspaper interviews, 'I think it's very sensible not to let people know what you're like.' At first sight this statement sits oddly with the pervasive presence of the 'I' figure in his poetry. All but half a dozen of the poems in *The Less Deceived* are related by an 'I' figure, a persona, and more than half the poems in *The Whitsun Weddings* and *High Windows* fall into the same category. Why should such a private man have chosen to speak with such a public flourish of the first person?

It is not easy to answer that question, though in some cases there are no problems. Larkin adopts from time to time a voice so obviously different from his own that his satiric or ironic purposes are in no doubt. It gives him a mischievous enjoyment to pretend to be the smug, trendy left-wing lecturer in 'Naturally the Foundation will Bear Your Expenses' (*The Whitsun Weddings*), flying out of London on Armistice Sunday:

> That day when Queen and Minister
> And Band of Guards and all
> Still act their solemn-sinister
> Wreath-rubbish in Whitehall.
>
> It used to make me throw up,
> These mawkish nursery games:
> O when will England grow up?

That's clearly not the genuine Larkin, the conservative ritual-lover who celebrates the continuity of English tradition in 'Show Saturday' (*High Windows*): 'Let it always be there.' Nor is there any danger of identifying Larkin, the lifelong librarian, with the disillusioned ex-reader in 'A Study of Reading Habits' (*The Whitsun Weddings*) who proclaimed 'Books are a load of crap'.

There are very few occasions when Larkin assumes a persona as clearly as this, and it is tempting to dismiss the whole idea of personae and to accept that in the 'I' poems he is speaking to us directly in his own voice. Certainly there is some appearance of consistency in the topics he chooses to return to and his attitudes towards them: for instance, his reluctance to make a definite commitment to person or place:

> No, I have never found
> The place where I could say
> *This is my proper ground,*
> *Here I shall stay*
>
> ('Places, Loved Ones', *The Less Deceived*)

This uneasiness, this unwillingness to settle, recurs frequently; the very word 'home' evokes in Larkin the exact opposite of those snug and comfy emotions one is supposed to feel. 'Home is so sad' (*The Whitsun Weddings*) or:

> We all hate home
> And having to be there:
> I detest my room,
> Its specially-chosen junk,
> The good books, the good bed
>
> ('Poetry of Departures', *The Less Deceived*)

The voices pronouncing on these recurrent themes, however, vary subtly and sometimes the reactions of the 'I' figure are unexpectedly different. The good books, the good bed, the possessions that are so despised in the last poem would never have been rejected by the 'I' in 'Mr Bleaney' (*The Whitsun Weddings*), whose rented room contained the bare essentials:

> Bed, upright chair, sixty-watt bulb, no hook
>
> Behind the door, no room for books or bags

Larkin can't be speaking to us directly in both these poems. In fact, I don't think he is in either, though he is using the different personae to explore areas which concern him personally.

In 'Mr Bleaney' Larkin uses his persona very sparingly and subtly. As the poem progresses it would seem to be a portrait of the previous inhabitant of the room, Bleaney, and his irritating habits. We only realise who the poem is really about at the very end:

> But if he stood and watched the frigid wind
> Tousling the clouds, lay on the fusty bed
> Telling himself that this was home, and grinned,
> And shivered, without shaking off the dread
>
> That how we live measures our own nature,
> And at his age having no more to show
> Than one hired box should make him pretty sure
> He warranted no better, I don't know.

After the contorted syntax of these two verses the directness and simplicity of the last three words is devastating. Not only does 'I' not know whether Bleaney experienced the same claustrophobic misery and sense of failure, but he doesn't *know* ... at all.

This rich ambivalence must be one of Larkin's reasons for using so many 'I' spokesmen. It enables him to enter intimately into a situation while at the same time standing a little to one side. Of course, these situations come from Larkin's own life; the uncertainty of so many of the personae stems from an awareness of his own uncertainties. Poetically Larkin expands this into a series of slightly comic, bewildered figures:

> Strange to know nothing, never to be sure
> Of what is true or right or real,
> But forced to qualify *or so I feel*,
> Or *Well, it does seem so*:
> *Someone must know.*

('Ignorance', *The Whitsun Weddings*)

In a way such personae also act as a defence. They enable Larkin, 'without a chance of consequence', to expose some of those sore places, sore through continual rubbing. He can pre-empt criticism of his real self by mocking the attitudes of a fictional version of himself. In 'Self's the Man' (*The Whitsun Weddings*) Larkin invents a smug bachelor figure who laughs at a married acquaintance (with the slightly comic name of Arnold) saddled with wife and kiddies:

> On, no one can deny
> That Arnold is less selfish than I.
> He married a woman to stop her getting away
> Now she's there all day

The jaunty rhythm and some comic rhymes — 'houses' and 'trousers', for instance — stop us taking the persona too seriously, even when the note of uncertainty appears again at the end. 'I' decides that Arnold, in marrying, has followed his own desires:

> Playing his own game.
> So he and I are the same,
>
> Only I'm a better hand
> At knowing what I can stand
> Without them sending a van —
> Or I suppose I can.

When Larkin wants to explore the same area more seriously, he has only to slip into another, less obvious persona, more closely related to his own character. In 'Dockery and Son' (*The Whitsun Weddings*) the 'I' figure visits what sounds very much like an Oxford college — Larkin himself was at St John's, Oxford — and chats with the Dean. He is told that one of his contemporaries, Dockery, now has a son at the college. The tone of the opening of the poem is lightly ironic, gently mocking the 'I' figure who, 'death-suited', attempts to get into his old room only to find it locked and departs by train 'ignored'. The mildly comic failures of the whole expedition are encapsulated when he changes trains at Sheffield and eats 'an awful pie'. The reader is lulled by the lightness of tone. It is only the brilliant image of the railway lines in the moonlight that transforms the mood of the poem. The Larkin figure:

> . . . walked along
> The platform to its end to see the ranged
> Joining and parting lines reflect a strong
>
> Unhindered moon

reflecting on the different routes his life and Dockery's had taken. Almost without realising it (apparently!) he slips into consideration of the factors that shape our lives and concludes, with flat finality:

> Life is first boredom, then fear.
> Whether or not we use it, it goes,
> And leaves what something hidden from us chose,
> And age, and then the only end of age.

The bleak euphemism of the final line comes directly at us, with no protective screen of persona. That slightly funny figure has disappeared altogether and the use of the first person plural reminds us that we, too, are involved.

The same gradual effacement of the persona and drawing in of the reader occurs in one of Larkin's best-known poems, 'Church Going', from *The Less Deceived*. In the first two verses we are again presented with a mildly foolish figure, ignorant and out of place in his uncomfortable attempts to show an undirected sort of piety:

> Hatless, I take off
> My cycle-clips in awkward reverence

When he reads at the lectern much more loudly than meant, 'The echoes snigger briefly.' But the gawky visitor serves only to introduce a much more general consideration of the gradual obsolescence of churches and their function. The 'I' voice falls almost silent and when it briefly re-emerges in the penultimate verse, it is with a new dignity and serenity, apparent in both sense and rhythm:

> For, though I've no idea
> What this accoutred frowsty barn is worth,
> It pleases me to stand in silence here

By the final verse the 'I' figure is no longer necessary. Once again, we are invited to share in the conclusion — a considerably less uncomfortable experience than that of 'Dockery and Son':

> A serious house on serious earth it is,
> In whose blent air all our compulsions meet,
> Are recognised and robed as destinies.

Perhaps it's significant that in much of Larkin's most serious poetry the 'I' figure gives way to the more general 'we'. Nowhere is this better seen than in what is probably Larkin's most satisfying poem, 'The Whitsun Weddings' (*The Whitsun Weddings*). Right from the start the 'I' voice seems very close to Larkin's own. 'That Whitsun, I was late getting away' is a straightforwardly direct opening, colloquial and neutral. On the train journey south from Hull, Larkin does at first present himself with slight irony as a disenchanted observer of towns and 'Canals with floatings of industrial froth' and 'acres of dismantled cars'. But as the journey progresses, the noise of wedding parties at every station attracts his attention, and he catches sight of all the friends and relations stranded on the hot platforms as the newly-weds take off. Despite himself, he feels drawn in to it:

> Struck, I leant
> More promptly out next time, more curiously

As fresh couples climb aboard, Larkin seems to feel himself caught up in this 'frail/ Travelling coincidence'. The word 'we' recurs more and more frequently towards the end of the poem, as if his awareness of these couples, all blissfully unaware of each other's existence, gives him a brief feeling of community with them. This is strengthened by the compelling, obscure images of the last verse, full of strange fertility. As they approach the station, the train:

> and what it held
> Stood ready to be loosed with all the power
> That being changed can give. We slowed again,
> And as the tightened brakes took hold, there swelled
> A sense of falling, like an arrow-shower
> Sent out of sight, somewhere becoming rain.

'The Whitsun Weddings' seems the only poem where Larkin

lets himself be directly involved with his fellow-men without the distancing shield of a persona. By the end of the poem 'we' has taken over from 'I', or, rather, 'I' has become blended with 'we'. Larkin never again allows himself such direct commitment and communion. It is easier and more natural for him to hide his compassion, if that's not too strong a word, behind those 'I' figures which are only part Larkin. They share the follies and weaknesses of the rest of mankind, and, because he recognises those actual and potential weaknesses so clearly in himself, allow him to identify with his fellow human beings while still retaining his privacy. The personae of his poems seldom show their sympathy or compassion overtly, and it's always a tough sort of sympathy, sometimes masquerading as brutality. 'The Old Fools' in *High Windows* is full of invective for the incontinent idiocy of old age, but the bullying questions and the helpless anger are only building to the final, bleakly tender line when the disguise is dropped:

> Can they never tell
> What is dragging them back, and how it will end? Not at
> > night?
> Not when the strangers come? Never, throughout
> The whole hideous inverted childhood? Well,
> > We shall find out.

Once again, 'we' takes over from 'I', showing a universal rather than an individual concern. But as death and its approaches began to dominate Larkin's thoughts, so he found himself less and less able to express this concern in verse even through a persona. Cemetery Road had become a poetical as well as a literal cul-de-sac. He recognised this possibility 22 years before his death when he wrote, 'life is slow dying' and different ways of life:

> . . . advance
> On death equally slowly.
> And saying so to some
> Means nothing; others it leaves
> Nothing to be said.
> > ('Nothing to be Said', *The Whitsun Weddings*)

The always slender stream of writing slowed to a trickle.

In the last ten years of his life he only published three poems, wrote scarcely six more. The most important of the late productions explains exactly why:

> I work all day, and get half-drunk at night.
> Waking at four to soundless dark, I stare.
> In time the curtain-edges will grow light
> Till then I see what's really always there:
> Unresting death, a whole day nearer now,
> Making all thought impossible but how
> And where and when I shall myself die.
> Arid interrogation: yet the dread
> Of dying, and being dead,
> Flashes afresh to hold and horrify.

('Aubade')

Larkin stares out at us directly, nakedly. There is no unifying 'we' at the end of this poem. Death had come to seem aimed at him personally, and he couldn't stand ironically aside any more. He could no longer assume personae that were both him and a protection from himself. In the end, all the voices fell silent.

AFTERTHOUGHTS

1

How important is it to be able to identify a poet's 'own' voice (pages 72–73)?

2

Do you agree that the syntax of the extract from 'Mr Bleaney' quoted on page 74 is 'contorted'?

3

What tensions does Hallsmith identify in this essay between humour and seriousness in Larkin's poetry?

4

Do you agree that 'The Whitsun Weddings' is 'probably Larkin's most satisfying poem' (page 77)?

Roger Day

Roger Day is a Lecturer in the Department of Literature at the Open University, and the author of Larkin *(Open University Press, 1987).*

ESSAY

'That vast moth-eaten musical brocade': Larkin and religion

'Life is first boredom, then fear.' This bleak declaration towards the end of Larkin's poem 'Dockery and Son' (*The Whitsun Weddings*) expresses a view frequently to be found in Larkin's work — that existence is a meaningless phenomenon in which the only inevitability is death. Such an outlook can only be described as secular which, by dictionary definition, means 'non-religious' or 'non-ecclesiastical'. Yet, paradoxically, Larkin was associated to a considerable extent with matters of a religious nature in his lifetime: many of his friends were religious, and one of his best-known poems is entitled 'Church Going' (*The Less Deceived*). In this essay I shall examine this apparent contradiction in the course of discussing a number of poems from Larkin's three main collections. I shall also be suggesting in parts 1 and 2 a somewhat broader definition of the term 'religious' than simply taking it as synonymous with orthodox Christianity. (The exact etymology of 'religious' is obscure, though it is thought to be related to the Latin *religar*, meaning 'to bind fast to', i.e. relating to something outside or beyond the self.)

Larkin's interest in religious matters was lifelong and his family seems to have followed some practices commonly observed at that time by non-religious people: in a poem written in 1939 (not published in his lifetime) he recalls having 'grown up in shade of Church and State' and 'tea unsweet in Lent'. A schoolfriend, Noel Hughes, recalls that Larkin's father 'combined a total disbelief in Christianity with an admiration for the seemliness of Anglican ceremony on formal occasions, and with such seemliness he was buried'. Hughes goes on to recall that:

> Philip always kept his cards tight to his chest . . . it was during a sixth form history lesson that Philip passed a book under the table, pointed to a paragraph and hissed 'get out of that'. I believe the book to have been an early Joad and the paragraph set out the clear illogicality of any belief in God.
>
> ('The Young Mr Larkin', *Larkin at Sixty* — London, 1982–p. 22)

This episode notwithstanding, Larkin set to and wrote choruses in blank verse for a passion play for Holy Week in 1939 on behalf of a High Anglican schoolfriend. Perhaps this somewhat ambivalent attitude goes some way towards explaining the surprising fact, recorded after Larkin's death by a colleague at the University of Hull, that 'as a young man he had considered ordination in the Church of England', in spite of the fact that he 'never had any religious faith' but 'felt a reverence for the familiar forms of Anglican worship and would have liked to believe they rested on the truth'.[1] This may explain his attendance at Evensong at a local church: he was prompted initially by his friend the writer A N Wilson, who had on one occasion persuaded Larkin to go to a High Anglican service, whereupon he reported that he had 'tried to be devout, and really quite enjoyed it.'[2] It is Wilson's view that though Larkin sometimes said he'd 'love to be a believer', he was 'fundamentally anti-Christian' and 'did not like the idea of the demands which love

---

[1] A L Brett, 'Philip Larkin in Hull', *Philip Larkin 1922–1985. A Tribute*, ed. G Hartley (London, 1988), pp. 111–112.

[2] 'Philip Larkin', *The Spectator*, 7 December 1985, p. 24.

made either in a secular or a religious setting',[3] though love does feature in his work as we shall see later. (Larkin's own description of his position, on one occasion, was 'agnostic'.) Then, after his death, there was a certain irony in the way the nation paid tribute to a much-loved poet through the offices of the national church in the form of a 'Service In Memory of Philip Larkin C. H. C.B.E.' in Westminster Abbey on 14 February 1986. Admittedly, the service consisted mainly of 'non-religious' elements — a reading of several of his poems (including 'Church Going'), and performance of pieces by the jazz musicians Sidney Bechet and Bix Beiderbecke, though there was a Bidding Prayer at the beginning of the service which summed up the position rather neatly. It ran like this:

> In particular on this day we commemorate with thanksgiving Philip Larkin, who, possessing outstanding literary gifts, combined distinction with rare humility. We give thanks for his intellectual integrity which would not allow him to accept the consolations of a faith which he could not share and which would have delivered him from a fear of dying by which all his life he was haunted.

The words 'intellectual integrity' are worth lingering over, for they call to mind that Larkin was to some extent at one time part of the 'Movement' generation, those writers in the 1950s influenced by logical positivist philosophy who largely adopted a rationalist, sceptical attitude to life. Yet, as we shall see, this description in no way does full justice to Larkin's work which, though consciously secular in attitude, often reveals a far more complex and often rather awed approach to being alive.

1

The first group of poems I want to consider are those in which religion consciously figures. The most revealing pair are 'High Windows' and 'Church Going' (*The Less Deceived*), for both of

---

[3] BBC Radio 4, 9 October 1988.

them express a distinct, unambiguous rejection of religion as traditionally understood. (The 'I' in either poem is not necessarily Larkin, though it is reasonable to assume that to a great extent he is writing in his own person.) 'High Windows' (*High Windows*) is a poem about freedom and liberation: the narrator begins by describing the 'new' sexual freedom of a young couple, with the ironic comment that 'this is paradise'. This leads him then to ask himself whether when he was young an older generation had a similar perception of him, 'freedom' in his case being release from religious obligations — 'No God any more' — and worrying about damnation. So here, by implication, religion is seen initially as oppressive and guilt-inducing, something to be liberated from. (Yet is there not perhaps an ironical undertone to the image of the 'long slide' and the use of a mild swear word? For, if it were *true*, religion might provide reassurance?) The poem's most striking feature is the concluding stanza with the image of windows and light:

> Rather than words comes the thought of high windows:
> The sun-comprehending glass,
> And beyond it, the deep blue air, that shows
> Nothing, and is nowhere, and is endless.

This representation of liberation which is tied to no place or time or activity has an almost transcendental quality to it, expressing numinosity (i.e. a spiritual quality) and sense of awe. There is a mystical quality to it, a sense of going beyond the self. So, paradoxically, a poem which explicitly rejects orthodox religion calls for neo-religious language to describe its effect.

In a different way, something similar is true of the end of 'Church Going', though it has to be said at the outset that Larkin firmly insisted on its 'entirely secular' nature.[4] The title 'Church Going' is of course a pun, albeit a serious one: the poem describes a visit to a church, but it also expresses the conviction that church-going (that is, religious practice), is on the way out. It begins by describing a visit to a church, using the dramatic present tense. The narrator seems to experience

---

[4] Ian Hamilton, 'Four Conversations', *London Magazine*, vol. 4, no. 6, November 1964, p. 76.

ambivalent feelings — he experiences 'awkward reverence' yet is studiedly casual in the reference to 'some brass and stuff/ Up at the holy end.' The next four stanzas move into a reflective mode: what will happen when all churches fall 'out of use'? Will Christianity be followed by superstition, and then what follows *that*? Then, speculating on who the last person to visit the church will be, the narrator returns to himself and declares his pleasure in standing in the church, even though the 'religious' meaning of it in any supernatural sense escapes him. Yet the poem goes on to conclude in a sonorous, weighty and elevated style:

> A serious house on serious earth it is,
> In whose blent air all our compulsions meet,
> Are recognised, and robed as destinies.

The whole stanza, in Larkin's 'high' style, perfectly reflects the dignity of human life the lines recognise, and they are in marked contrast to the more colloquial style of earlier stanzas. The whole poem shows Larkin's characteristic care in selecting exactly the words he wants to achieve his effects: he went to the trouble of procuring the *Church Times* to get liturgical detail correct, and the pun on 'gravitating' in the final lines (i.e. grave, the Latin *gravitas*/ graves/gravitation) is masterly.

In this poem, Larkin appears willing to speak for a whole generation by the use of the plural forms 'we' and 'our' when pondering the use the churches will be put to. 'Church Going' has been widely anthologised and much discussed, and its appeal to an uneasily secular age where regular religious practice is the exception rather than the norm is not difficult to discern, for in this as with so many other of his subjects Larkin has distilled into memorable form what many have felt and continue to experience.

Larkin's resistance to those who would put a religious label on him is understandable for he is quite explicit in his rejection of a supernatural dimension to life. In 'Aubade', a poem published in *The Times Literary Supplement* (23 December 1977), religion is described as:

> That vast moth-eaten musical brocade
> Created to pretend we never die

Further evidence is to be found in another powerful poem about death, 'The Building' (*High Windows*), which employs religious imagery and then deliberately uses it for a secular purpose. The poem is about sickness and death, for the building of the title is, in a literal sense, a hospital. The patients (the word means 'those suffering') are described as 'unseen congregations' who are visited each evening and brought 'wasteful, weak, propitiatory' flowers. The conjunction of the adjectives 'wasteful' and 'propitiatory' is especially telling, for the latter is, among other usages, a theological term relating to an act of atonement (usually that of Christ). As the word 'wasteful' makes clear, here the gesture is plainly ineffective, for the 'powers' of the building clearly do *not* 'outbuild cathedrals', as the narrator speculates in the final lines, and, indeed, 'All know they are going to die'. What was Larkin's purpose in employing this 'religious' image? Perhaps precisely to make the point later to appear in 'Aubade', that the claim of religions to transcend death is simply untrue.

The fascination that the subject of religion had for Larkin is evident in his poem 'Water' (*The Whitsun Weddings*) where he ruminates on the part the element water would play if he were asked 'To construct a religion'. The 'liturgy' ('form of service'), Larkin's own choice of word, would centre on a 'devout drench'. Now Larkin must have known full well that his own phrase was a colloquial description of the basis of Christian life — the Sacrament of Baptism, or 'wetting the baby's head'. So, though there is an implicit rejection of existing religions (a new one has to be 'constructed'), at the same time we are presented with a 'secular' version of Christianity. Furthermore, in the final stanza, water in a glass would be turned to the East (which saw the birth of Christianity):

> Where any-angled light
> Would congregate endlessly.

In these lines we find not only the pun on 'congregate'/congregations but also intimations of light and eternity — qualities theologians will tell you possessed ineffably by God. They are also often to be found expressed in Larkin's poetry, especially in concluding lines.

2

For all the preoccupation with death, a subject Larkin wrote about frequently and powerfully, there is another side to his work which reveals a great sensitivity to, and love of, life. It is present even in a poem like 'The Building' in apposition to the main theme, and it is to be found more directly in poems of my second group which I am tempted to call 'secular hymns', though I suspect Larkin would not have accepted the term. ('Hymn', a Greek word, simply means 'song of praise'.) In first place in this 'group' I would place 'Solar' (*High Windows*), a poem which Larkin himself remarked was 'unlike anything I'd written for twenty years'[5] 'Solar' is a meditation, a disquisition on the nature of the sun, that life-sustaining centre of the part of the galaxy which we inhabit, and the poem conveys an awed, visionary sense of the wonder of it. It begins with the language of the nursery (the sun is a 'lion face'), moves through scientific description ('Continuously exploding' — the sun is in fact nuclear fusion, turning hydrogen into helium), and concludes with a recognition of its beneficence in meeting our needs which:

> Climb and return like angels.

The simile here is an interesting choice, for angels, however 'secular' in nature, are traditionally known as messengers of God, and the poem as a whole does acknowledge in broad terms a dependence on a greater power. I would even argue that it bears a resemblance to Psalm 103 which contains the following lines:

> All of these look to you
> To give them their food in due season.
> You gave it, they gather it up;
> You open your hand, they have their fill.
> (*A New Translation* — London, 1966)

Another poem of this kind is 'The Trees' (*High Windows*) which

---

[5] John Hafenden, *Viewpoints: Poets in Conversation* (London, 1981), p. 128.

expresses the recognition that each year, coming into leaf, trees play:

> Their yearly trick of looking new

The lines carry again a note of awe, a surprised recognition of the beauty of creation. The middle section of 'Livings' (*High Windows*) also has something of this quality, when a lighthouse keeper reflects in his solitude on the crashing world outside his isolated place of work which is also his home. Other poems simply record with quiet satisfaction a sense of a place or occasion. 'To the Sea' (*High Windows*) is a poem of this kind: the narrator, relishing his solitude ('happy at being on my own') observes with great sensitivity the ritual family behaviour on the beach and derives from it the feeling that this is how things should be:

> It may be that through habit these do best,
> Coming to water clumsily undressed
> Yearly; teaching their children by a sort
> Of clowning; helping the old, too, as they ought.

'Dublinesque' (*High Windows*), as the title suggests, is an evocation of the Irish city: its subject or focus is a passing funeral procession, but by building detail on to this, the narrator captures with the lightest touch the feel of a strange place and people. In this respect it is a little like 'The Importance of Elsewhere' (*The Whitsun Weddings*) which is also about the strangeness of being 'Lonely in Ireland, since it was not home'.

Finally, there is that great love of Larkin's life — early twentieth century jazz. Cedric Watts has written elsewhere in this book on this topic (pages 20–27), so I shall restrict myself simply to pointing out how 'For Sidney Bechet' (*The Whitsun Weddings*) celebrates with an authentic enthusiasm the enormous pleasure Larkin found in that kind of music. Mostly he wrote about it in prose in his reviews for the *Daily Telegraph*, and the note of pleasure carries clearly to the reader.

At the heart of these 'secular hymns' is a sense not simply of awe but also of thankfulness, whether so expressed as in 'Solar' or not. There is also an awareness of the mystery of being, and it is this which I shall take as the focus for poems in my third category.

3

If a label be needed, perhaps 'ontological' is the word for this final group. Ontology is a branch of metaphysics concerned with the study of being. Larkin clearly had a vivid sense of the 'million-petalled flower/ Of being here', as he puts it in 'The Old Fools' (*High Windows*) and it was precisely this that rendered death such a fearful prospect. Larkin's sense of 'being here' emerges quite often in poems which are ostensibly about something else — 'High Windows' is an example, initially about sexual liberation but ending in an eternity of sun and sky. A poem more specifically directed to ontological matters is simply entitled 'Here' (*The Whitsun Weddings*). 'Here' begins on a train and describes a journey through countryside to an estuary town, fairly clearly Hull from the mention of a 'slave museum'. The middle stanzas describe the life of the people of the town ('urban yet simple') and this forms a preface, contrasting with the final verse which is set in:

> Isolate villages, where removed lives
>
> Loneliness clarifies. Here silence stands
> Like heat.

(The syntax of these lines is not easy to grasp at first; 'clarifies' the verb and its subject 'loneliness' follow the object they modify — 'loneliness clarifies removed lives' would be the more usual sequence.) In contrast to the town people, the speaker in this final stanza glories in solitude and:

> . . . unfenced existence,
> Facing the sun, untalkative, out of reach.

The verbs used are all ones of life and growth in this final stanza — 'flower', 'thicken', 'quicken' — and so the impression created is positive; solitude is not presented as isolated sterility but as something good. As in 'High Windows', the images are of light and air, so that existence is to be enjoyed and rejoiced in. A religious person might well think of the psalmist's line:

> I thank you for the wonder of my being
> (Psalm 138, *A New Translation*)

and Larkin's lines seem a 'secular' equivalent of this, though whether he would have agreed is perhaps open to doubt. 'Absences' (*The Less Deceived*) is a much earlier poem which is also about 'being here', though less a celebration than 'Here' and more philosophical in nature. It was a favourite poem of Larkin's and he sent it as such to a collection called *Poet's Choice*. It consists mainly of images of rain and sea which then shift to the open sky, and finally to:

> Such attics cleared of me! Such absences!

So, using methods reminiscent of French symbolist poets, Larkin conveys a powerful sense of presence but does so by inversion, imagining his own *non*-existence. Another poem in the same collection, 'Dry-Point', though principally about post-coital disillusion, ends with an image depicting the speaker's intensely private world, again employing light:

> And how remote that bare sunscrubbed room.
> Intensely far, that padlocked cube of light
> We neither define nor prove,
> Where you, we dream, obtain no right of entry.

The inference to be drawn from the third line of this stanza is surely that life can only be 'experienced' — its *meaning* is impossible to pin down. This appears to be the position Larkin maintained until his death, though the quality of 'experiencing' appears to have become richer. You can see this in a poem like 'Show Saturday' (*High Windows*), a wonderfully funny and acutely observed poem about a country show which is full of memorable detail and phrases, such as these describing members of a family:

> Children all saddle-swank, mugfaced middleaged wives
> Glaring at jellies, husbands on leave from the garden
> Watchful as weasels, car-tuning curt-haired sons —

'To the Sea' (*High Windows*) shows similar traits and is narrated by the solitary observer who, nonetheless, is participating in a communal day of relaxation simply by his watching presence. All the more poignant, then, was Larkin's despairing remark to Andrew Motion (his official biographer) during his last illness: '*Well I've nothing to live for*', as recorded in the latter's poem of tribute, 'This Is Your Subject Speaking'.

Throughout Larkin's poetry there is a continuing interest (however agnostic) in the nature of human existence. In this sense, Larkin had his own rather English, rather empirical interest in metaphysics, though it would be wrong to call him a 'philosophical poet'. It is not right, either, to call him a 'religious' poet, though the number of times religion, or religious concerns in the broader sense outlined at the beginning of this essay, comes into the poems is surprising. Sometimes this takes the form simply of using certain words and phrases: for example, '(priced/ Far above rubies)' in 'For Sidney Bechet' (*The Whitsun Weddings*) is biblical ('A virtuous woman who can find?/ For her price is far above rubies' — Proverbs 31: 10). 'Ambulances' (*The Whitsun Weddings*) begins with the line 'Closed like confessionals'. 'Faith Healing' (*The Whitsun Weddings*) is more explicitly about the failure of religion, in this case as mediated through an American healer, to console. What has damaged the old ladies who figure in 'Faith Healing' is a lack of being loved, which 'nothing cures', and love is another subject which occurs throughout Larkin's work.

In this respect, Larkin makes me think of W H Auden (whom he imitated in his youth). Auden *was* a 'religious' poet in his later years and is responsible for the memorable line:

> We must love one another or die.

Perhaps Larkin's equivalent line is the conclusion of 'An Arundel Tomb' (*The Whitsun Weddings*):

> What will survive of us is love

which he qualifies as 'almost true'. But note the number of other places where Larkin mentions love: in *The Less Deceived* it occurs most frequently in the 'romantic' sense in poems like 'Lines on a Young Lady's Photograph Album' or 'No Road'. In *The Whitsun Weddings* the subject is considered in the wider sense: 'Faith Healing' contains the unforgettable lines:

> In everyone there sleeps
> A sense of life lived according to love.

The difficulties inherent in trying to live this way are described in other poems in the collection: in 'Love Songs in Age' 'that much-mentioned brilliance, love' fails to console the widow; in 'The Large Cool Store' love is 'separate and unearthly'; while in 'Wild Oats' the narrator realises wanly that he is 'too selfish' to be able to love. It is worth recording, too, A N Wilson's report of what Larkin liked in a book of diaries he had lent him. He valued them for the way they evoked 'a bygone bachelor world — sticks in the varnished hall stand, lodgings, walking tours . . . And of course tremendous inarticulate love'. As Wilson observes, the comment seems to encapsulate something of Larkin himself.[6] Now I would not want to say that, because he wrote about love, Larkin was, whether he knew it or not, 'religious' (on the grounds of the traditional teaching 'Ubi caritas, Deus est' — where love is, there is God), but it is never-theless the case that there are qualities in his work which have a certain familiarity to the religiously minded. He wrote of light, love, freedom, eternity — qualities attributed by people of all religions to God. (Seamus Heaney has remarked on this quality of light in Larkin's work, and A N Wilson in his obituary hoped, in a memorable phrase, that he would be 'blinking his eyes on the edge of paradise'.) He wrote of the mystery of being, with a sense of wonder at creation — again, experiences familiar to those with religious beliefs in the widest sense. Yet, at the same time, he has rightly been accused of pessimism, deep sadness and despair and he was quite explicit in his rejection of the belief of orthodox or traditional religion, though it seems that he valued Anglican liturgical practice, perhaps because of its 'Englishness'. Larkin's relationship with religion was thus less straightforward than his forthright rejection suggests. And his work continues to generate a variety of responses, as you will have noticed if you compare mine with that, say, of Graham Holderness (pages 106–114). But this very diversity, it seems to me, is proof of the richness and complexity of feeling to be found in Larkin's poetry.

---

[6] *The Spectator*, 7 December 1985, p. 24.

AFTERTHOUGHTS

1

What paradox does Day identify at the beginning of this essay? To what extent is he able to resolve it by the arguments that follow?

2

Consider the importance of imagery of light in Larkin's poetry, in relation to Day's comments on page 86.

3

Discuss the relevance to this essay of the quotation cited in its title.

4

Compare this essay with the essays by Hollindale on pages 50–60 and by Draper on pages 95–104. What similarities and differences do you find?

Ronald Draper

Ronald Draper is Regius Professor of Literature at the University of Aberdeen, and the author of numerous scholarly publications.

ESSAY

The positive Larkin[1]

> Only one ship is seeking us, a black-
> Sailed unfamiliar, towing at her buck
> A huge and birdless silence. In her wake
> No waters breed or break.

('Next Please', *The Less Deceived*)

To many readers this is the typical Larkinian theme. This ship is, of course, the ship of death, symbolically 'black-Sailed' and familiar from long literary tradition, but '*un*familiar', too, because of its strange accompaniments — not the usual dinghy and birds eager for scraps of food behind it, but 'silence' and lifeless, motionless water. Larkin here makes one of the great commonplaces of poetry seem chillingly new to us, while remaining what it is — a universal human experience. Because he often dwells on this theme of mortality, as in 'Ambulances' (*The Whitsun Weddings*), 'The Old Fools' and 'The Building' (*High Windows*) and 'Aubade', all of which are powerful, relent-

---

[1] The work of several commentators on Larkin has influenced me in this essay, but I would like to make special acknowledgement of my debt to J R Watson's seminal article, 'The Other Larkin' in *Critical Quarterly 17*, no. 4, Winter 1975, pp. 347–360.

lessly honest poems about the inevitability of death, and because in poems like 'No Road' (*The Less Deceived*), 'Love Songs in Age' and 'Dockery and Son' (*The Whitsun Weddings*) he seems to question the value of such things as love and family life which for many people are the necessary counterbalance to death, he is thought of as a gloomy, despondent, negative poet.

Yet this is only one half of Larkin. The other half is a more positive poet who celebrates habits and customs which make life civilised and satisfyingly worth living, and who is an English provincial poet with a deeply patriotic (though not crudely jingoistic) feeling for his native country. Sometimes what appears to be presented negatively is only the reverse aspect of a positive theme, as, for example, in 'Going, Going' (*High Windows*), the title of which is taken from the auctioneer's cry: 'Going, going, gone'. This poem (rather unusually, for Larkin, an 'occasional' poem, commissioned by the Department of the Environment in 1972) is a sardonically morose commentary on the way twentieth-century materialism is leading to developmental eyesores, overcrowding and pollution, with the prospect of everything being 'bricked in' till the land will qualify as 'First slum of Europe'. The vision seems bleak:

> And that will be England gone,
> The shadows, the meadows, the lanes,
> The guildhalls, the carved choirs.
> There'll be books; it will linger on
> In galleries; but all that remains
> For us will be concrete and tyres.

The first three lines of this penultimate stanza, however, point to the poet's strong feeling for what is being threatened. The contempt expressed in 'concrete and tyres' is as intense as it is precisely *because* of the love felt for England's countryside and the beauty of its architectural inheritance.

Another poem with the word 'going' in its title, 'Church Going' (*The Less Deceived*), is highly relevant to this theme. (There is also a third one, called simply 'Going', which, it must be admitted, in its own words, 'brings no comfort'.) Here, too, a superficial reading, especially of the earlier stanzas, can make Larkin appear misleadingly negative. As he steps into the church (on a weekday — for the decorative flowers, 'cut/ For

Sunday', are 'brownish now') his attitude seems mockingly detached, and the language of the early part of the poem is, if not jeeringly satirical, at least flippant: '*sprawlings* of flowers', 'some brass and *stuff*', the heavy-print Bible has '*Hectoring* large-scale verses', and when the poet pronounces 'Here endeth' the echoes '*snigger* briefly'. But already there is something in the atmosphere which affects him in spite of himself, as hinted in the triple epithets of line 7: 'And a tense, musty, unignorable silence'. The negative form, '*un*ignorable', gently insists on a silence which cannot be disregarded. Similarly, the mocking gesture for which this poem has become notorious ('Hatless, I take off/ My cycle-clips in awkward reverence'), while being comic, is nevertheless indicative of some sort of pressure which he feels to show respect. The reverence is indeed 'awkward' — a product of ineptitude, but also of real, if not as yet properly understood, feeling.

At the beginning of the third stanza the superficial idea that the place 'was not worth stopping for' (last line of stanza 2) is countered by 'Yet stop I did: in fact I often do'; and a process of 'wondering' is initiated which still includes some of the earlier mild mockery ('cathedrals *chronically* on show', for example, line 24) and for a while retains the note of scepticism, especially with regard to the superstitious uses to which the poet imagines the disused church being put, but which gradually descends into deeper and deeper waters till firm bottom is at last reached with the great themes (universal and traditional commonplaces once more) of 'marriage, and birth,/ And death, and thoughts of these' (11.50–51). The attitude of mocking detachment still makes itself felt (for example, in the disparaging reference to the church as 'this accoutred frowsty barn', line 52), but in the last stanzas this mood is thrown off altogether. The poet becomes completely 'serious' (it is his own chosen and deliberately repeated word), and the poetry becomes that of solemn (but in no way pompous) statement, resonant with a final recognition of the perennial human need which not only this particular church, but the universal Church — the very notion of institutionalised religion as such — has existed to satisfy in the past and will continue to satisfy for someone in the future:

A serious house on serious earth it is,
In whose blent air all our compulsions meet,
Are recognised, and robed as destinies.
And that much never can be obsolete,
Since someone will forever be surprising
A hunger in himself to be more serious,
And gravitating with it to this ground,
Which, he once heard, was proper to grow wise in,
If only that so many dead lie round.

This transitional technique, as it might be called — the process by which a change gradually takes place from detached scepticism and mockery, or bored indifference, to a deeper recognition of underlying truths, or traditional, shared values — is characteristic of several of Larkin's finest poems. It is there, for example, in 'The Whitsun Weddings' (*The Whitsun Weddings*), where a hot, tired and initially uninterested traveller boards a train bound from a northern provincial city to London. (We easily identify the traveller as Larkin himself journeying on a Saturday afternoon from Hull to King's Cross, but the poem is full of such graphic, novel-like detail that it creates its own atmosphere independently of any personal, biographical reference.) At first he does not notice the wedding parties and newly married couples gathered at the stations where the train stops; and when he does become aware of their presence his attitude is that of a somewhat satirically aloof spectator, seeing the girls, for example, as 'grinning and pomaded' and dressed in 'parodies of fashion' (11.28–29). But then his attention is caught, and 'Struck', he says, 'I leant/ More promptly out next time, more curiously'. He still sees cheapness and vulgarity in the fathers with 'seamy foreheads', the mothers 'loud and fat' and 'An uncle shouting smut', but now he begins to note how their wedding outfits 'Marked off the girls unreally from the rest' (1.41). His point of view shifts nearer to theirs, and he begins to enter into their feelings, and also those of the wedding guests, and in particular to appreciate the more serious emotions that lie beneath the tawdry surface:

> The women shared
> The secret like a happy funeral;

D

> While girls, gripping their handbags tighter, stared
> At a religious wounding.

Through such language the weddings acquire a sense of ritual, and the poet himself becomes a tacit participant rather than a merely detached observer. With a telling eye for detail he still notes the commonplace features of the outside scene as the train approaches the terminus, but the sharing of human beings in a significant act which changes their lives is what becomes the focus of the poem. And with this almost imperceptible raising of the imaginative temperature comes an intensification of the poem's imagery. For example, London's numbered postal districts register in the mind of the now thoroughly awakened poet as 'packed like squares of wheat', conveying a suggestion of fertility and harvest which makes its own unspoken contribution to the now deepened significance of the weddings; and the delicately observed sensation of being pitched forward as the train brakes at the entrance to the final station becomes, daringly, 'like an arrow-shower/ Sent out of sight, somewhere becoming rain', in which it is not too much to perceive a hint of a phallic and appropriately procreative consummation to the journey. The last word of that image (which is also the very last word of the poem) emphasises the cool, fertilising and sympathetic power of 'rain', as opposed to the hot, arid mood of indifference in which the poem had started, and so completes the carefully nurtured process of transition.

If it seems an exaggeration to attach such significance to the word 'rain' at the end of 'The Whitsun Weddings', it is worth considering the short poem called 'Water' which immediately precedes it in *The Whitsun Weddings* volume. The tone of 'Water' is, admittedly, not easy to ascertain: it seems a curious blend of playfulness and seriousness. The ritualistic elements in 'Church Going' and 'The Whitsun Weddings' are also present in this poem in what seem to be *un-ironic*, references to 'a religion', 'Going to church', 'liturgy', and, in the last stanza, the raising of a chalice as in an act of communion. But, on the other hand, the supposition that 'I' might be 'called in/ To construct a religion' is more than absurd (as if one could do it like constructing a bridge), and the devised rituals sound like adolescent horse-play, especially in stanza three:

My liturgy would employ
Images of sousing,
A furious devout drench.

If these seeming incompatibles can be reconciled, perhaps it is via the sense of religion as something that can be entered into joyously, recapturing a lost childish innocence. The element of water is common to both moods: symbolic of spiritual renewal (as in baptism by immersion in water), it is also a simple, elemental liquid to splash about in and to admire for its wonderful light effects.

A similar combination of ordinary pleasure with an almost ritualistic sense of the significance of water occurs in another, highly positive poem of Larkin's — 'To the Sea' (*High Windows*). Here he writes tenderly, and yet without sentimentality, on the subject of visiting the seaside. Memories of his own childhood holidays when he searched for cigarette cards in the sands ('I searched the sand for Famous Cricketers') mingle with the 1970s reality of transistor radios blaring out over the beach (though being out of doors they don't sound impossibly noisy), and 'uncertain children, frilled in white/ And grasping at enormous air' share the seaside experience with the 'rigid old' in wheelchairs. It is, in a natural, loose, unorganised way, a communal experience, and one which in the last, climactic stanza, the poet not only gives his blessing to, but also derives a moral lesson from:

                    If the worst
Of flawless weather is our falling short,
It may be that through habit these do best,
Coming to water clumsily undressed
Yearly; teaching their children by a sort
Of clowning; helping the old, too, as they ought.

The alliteration of 'flawless' and 'falling' draws attention to the contrast between the ideal of perfection (traditionally expressed in terms of a golden age or a prelapsarian paradise, but here quite simply a matter of perfect summer weather) and the *im*perfection of fallen man, with the consequently deeply felt need of a ritual which can in some way bridge the gap between the two, and which is again associated, as in so many religions and in some of the Larkin poems already discussed, with 'water'. Yet the hint of ritual is as remote from pompous ceremony or esoteric mystery as it could possibly be. On the contrary, it is founded in nothing more unusual than the annual interruption of routine work which takes ordinary families for a week or fortnight's holiday by the sea, but involves them in another form of 'habit' and the fulfilment of duties to young and old which constitute an unpretentious and unselfconscious form of virtue. The water has a redemptive power (or, as Larkin more cautiously expresses it, 'It may be' that it has), not through its magic or divine qualities, but simply by its being the accepted focus of a communal event.

'To the Sea' is the opening poem of Larkin's last published volume of verse, *High Windows* — a volume in which, despite the presence of 'The Old Fools' and 'The Building', his positive awareness of varieties of communal experience seems to be greater than ever before. Thus, the remarkable trio of poems entitled 'Livings' presents three quite different patterns of life: no. I concerns the recurrent visit of an agricultural salesman to 'The ——— Hotel in ——— ton for three days', no. II the solitary existence of a lighthouse keeper, and no. III the dining customs of a group of eighteenth-century Oxbridge dons. There is something stale in the routine of no. I, as its last line suggests: 'It's time for change, in nineteen twenty-nine'; and complacency can be felt in the banal subjects of conversation that fill no. III. But the primitive strength (again associated with the sea and the sea-world) of the images in no. II is a reminder of elemental powers which continue to exist as a reservoir of energy, and their positioning between the other two poems seems to vitalise the neighbouring portraits.

'The Card-Players' is an equally remarkable poem, both in subject-matter and structure. It evokes characters lifted from the world of those seventeenth-century Dutch interior painters who presented the lives of crude, unsophisticated peasants in vividly, realistic detail. Here, with such comically crude names as 'Jan von Hogspeuw' 'Dirk Dogstoerd' (obviously pronounced 'turd') and 'Old Prijck' they express an unembarrassed relish for physical pleasures which communicates both revolting coarseness and immense vitality. The whole poem is, somewhat unexpectedly, a sonnet rhyming *abbacddcefeggf*, and divided, not into the usual octave and sestet (8 lines and 6), but 13 lines and one final, isolated line which sums up the elemental forces that have been faithfully copied in the preceding lines: 'Rain, wind and fire! The secret, bestial peace!'

To those who know Larkin only from his more seemingly morose poems 'The Card-Players' is a surprise. Another such poem is 'Dublinesque'. Here Larkin almost jauntily evokes the totally un-funereal jollity of an Irish funeral which happily combines 'an air of great friendliness' with one 'of great sadness also'. He creates a communal pattern which is distinctly non-English (as is that of 'The Card-Players'), but which contributes via its two-stressed dancing rhythm to the recurrent impression created in *High Windows* that Larkin is fascinated by individuals and groups whose pattern of life reflects something greater and more powerful than their own merely private selves.

From this point of view the most important poem in *High Windows* is 'Show Saturday'. The show is an explicitly communal occasion, bringing together a diversity of people in a diversity of activities, including dog, pony and sheep competitions, log-sawing, a wrestling match, pony-jumping and displays of vegetables, dairy produce, cooking, handicraft and needlework — all meticulously detailed and properly appreciated for their 'skills'. There are also side-shows, clothes stalls, a beer tent, lavatories and a bank. The whole place is full of bustling, jostling business and pleasure mixed, and the simplest, plainest poetry of things suffices to express its ordinary excellences:

> blanch leeks like church candles, six pods of
> Broad beans (one split open), dark shining-leafed cabbages —
> rows
> Of single supreme versions, followed (on laced
> Paper mats) by dairy and kitchen; four brown eggs, four white
> eggs,
> Four plain scones, four dropped scones . . .

As an occasion it is a remarkable example of unity in multiplicity. But only a temporary one. Already in stanza 5, with the pony events still going on, horse-boxes are starting to move, and in stanzas 6–8 a process of disintegration takes place which dissolves the temporary unity back into its separate, higgledy-piggledy component parts, and sends the participants back to their 'private addresses, gates and lamps/ In high stone one-street villages, empty at dusk,/ And side roads of small towns' (11.43–45). As this happens the poetry becomes (especially in stanza 7) more sardonic, reverting to that mockingly detached Larkinian style which is characteristic of the earlier parts of 'Church Going' and 'The Whitsun Weddings'. For example, children showing off with their ponies are satirically dismissed as 'all saddle-swank', house-proud women become 'mugfaced middleaged wives/ Glaring at jellies' and motor-obsessed youths are neatly summed up as 'car-tuning curt-haired sons'. Crudeness, boastfulness, even swindling (1.60) re-assert themselves as routine parts of the people's 'local lives' (1.53); they become their normal, unregenerate selves once more. This is not cynicism, however, for 'the dismantled Show' (and its intimation of a finer unity) is something which remains behind the banal façade of everyday life as a potentiality capable of renewal. Or, to be more precise, in his closing lines the poet — changing from the indicative mood of straightforward description to the subjunctive mood of wishing, almost, indeed, of prayer — commends the idea of renewal, and urges it upon the reader, as if to suggest that the Show is a form of annual ritual which enacts for us the possibility of a deeply needed communal union:

> Let it stay hidden there like strength, below
> Sale-bills and swindling; something people do,
> Not noticing how time's rolling smithy-smoke
> Shadows much greater gestures; something they share
> That breaks ancestrally each year into
> Regenerate union. Let it always be there.

In those final lines the language has shed its sardonic touches again and replaced them with words like 'ancestrally' and 'regenerate' which have powerfully religious associations. Yet Larkin was not a religious man, in the sense of one who subscribes to a religious faith. His creed was bleakly agnostic (as he makes absolutely plain in the remorselessly honest poem, 'Aubade', published in the The Times Literary Supplement in 1977). In which respect it is as well to note that the theme of mortality and the eroding force of time, mentioned at the beginning of this essay as a generally accepted feature of Larkin's poetry, is also present in these lines from 'Show Saturday'. The image of the 'rolling smithy-smoke' is an ominous one, and it threatens 'much greater gestures' than these of the annual 'Show'. The poet has not forgotten the inevitability of death and annihilation, and he tacitly admits that the vital potentiality he wishes to find in the show may not really be capable of effecting the 'Regenerate union' he longs for. The important thing, however, is that he sees something worthwhile in its simple pleasures and that he would have us build on them, if we can. He would bolster a tradition which at least offers the chance of counteracting the destructive elements inherent in the human condition.

Briefly, as a postscript, it is also worth mentioning the exceptionally beautiful poem which appears as the last one in *High Windows* — 'The Explosion'. This is written in the curiously jog-trot metre of Longfellow's poem on the American Indian, Hiawatha (though Larkin very skilfully controls his rhythms so that the lines do not sound as banal as Longfellow's are apt to do), and the effect is to give the poem a naive, slightly unreal air. The theme is once more death. In the first half of the poem a group of miners are shown on their way to the pit-head; one chases a rabbit and comes back with 'a nest of lark's eggs'. It could almost be a scene from *Sons and Lovers*. An explosion occurs, described only in terms of its surface 'tremor', and then, in the second half of the poem, which opens with biblical words expressing a belief in resurrection, the widowed wives of the miners are presented as having a vision in which they see their husbands:

> Larger than in life they managed —
> Gold as on a coin, or walking
> Somehow from the sun towards them,
>
> One showing the eggs unbroken.

The Easter symbolism of the eggs is a strong, positive note at the end, heightened in effect by the printing of the line on its own as a final, one-line stanza; and it creates a remarkably positive conclusion to the whole *High Windows* volume. If it does not cancel out all that has gone before — including, as I have already noted, the very different sense of decay and mortality in 'The Old Fools' and 'The Building' — it reminds us of the Larkin who, though he could not himself subscribe to a religious faith, was well able to understand the very human need for religious communion, and was capable of giving deeply moving expression to that need.

AFTERTHOUGHTS

1

How 'patriotic' (page 95) do you find Larkin's poetry?

2

Do you agree with Draper's arguments regarding the significance of water in Larkin's poetry (pages 98–100)?

3

Explain the importance to Draper's argument of his analysis of 'Show Saturday' (pages 101–103).

4

Compare this essay with the essays by Hollindale on pages 50–60 and by Day on pages 81–92. What similarities and differences do you find?

E

Graham Holderness

Graham Holderness is Head of the Drama Department at the Roehampton Institute of Higher Education, and has published numerous works of criticism.

ESSAY

Philip Larkin: the limits of experience

'Larkin's poetry of lowered sights and patiently diminished expectations can be justified.'[1]

Philip Larkin's verse is a poetry of simplicity. That does not mean simple-mindedness, since it is everywhere characterised by subtlety, wit, irony, intelligence; but it has the transparency of a poetry content to use the common language of spoken communication as the basis of its diction. The use of common speech, colloquial vocabulary and easily intelligible syntax, gives Larkin's a verse quality of accessibility uncommon in twentieth-century poetry.

The common language is an appropriate voice: for Larkin's poetry is designed to be, above all, a poetry of common life and common experience, of the kind he himself admired in Thomas Hardy:

> ... when I came to Hardy it was with a sense of relief that I didn't have to try to jack myself up to a concept of poetry that lay outside my own life — and this is perhaps what I felt Yeats

---

[1] Donald Davie, *Thomas Hardy and British Poetry* (London, 1972), p. 71.

was trying to make me do. One could simply relapse back into one's own life and write from it. Hardy taught me to feel rather than to write — of course one has to use one's own language and one's own jargon and one's own situations — and he taught one as well to have confidence in what one felt.

('Philip Larkin praises the poetry of Thomas Hardy', *The Listener*, 25 July 1968, p. 111)

The position described here is a strong and respectable one in English poetry: it was Wordsworth's, and few people would want to dissent from Larkin's admiration of Hardy. But there is one phrase in that quotation that strikes an individual note, more typical of Larkin himself, and it is a trait that will require further investigation. Neither Wordsworth nor Hardy would have spoken about 'relapsing back' into ordinary life as the characteristic stance of the poet. This passage can be regarded as a key to the strengths and weaknesses of Larkin's poetry, and to the question of whether 'lowered sights' and 'diminished expectations', where they appear to be attitudes of the poet's rather than simply part of his subject-matter, are conducive to the production of an effective and creative kind of poetry.

1

The relationship between a poet's 'technique' and his 'philosophy' is at the heart of the problem. Larkin speaks about poetic form in much the same way as he characterises his attitude to life: the keynote being 'acceptance':

The kind of poetry I've enjoyed has been the kind of poetry you'd associate with me, Hardy pre-eminently, Wilfred Owen, Auden, Christina Rossetti, William Barnes; on the whole, people to whom technique seems to matter less than content, people who accept the forms they have inherited, but use them to express their own content.

(from Ian Hamilton, 'Four Conversations', *London Magazine*, IV:6, November 1964, p. 71)

In keeping with this emphasis, Larkin's conception of an ideal audience is anti-intellectual and anti-academic: he prefers an audience of 'ordinary' people with whom he (as an 'ordinary' person) could identify: people who read poetry spontaneously, for pleasure; who are more interested in 'feeling' and 'content' than in 'technique' and 'form'; and who would find in Larkin's own poems an honest and truthful reflection of their own experience.

Larkin aimed then by his own admission to write a poetry of a comprehensible kind, in clear, colloquial language and familiar poetic forms, with a minimum of verbal, syntactical and metaphorical experiment; a poetry which could serve as a medium for expressing the 'ordinary', the common, the everyday experiences of his own contemporary society. His larger claim was that the experiences he described were representative, and constituted an honest portrayal of human life in a particular social and cultural condition. Larkin's admirers have suggested that his observations on life were wholly representative of the mood and feeling of the 1940s and 50s, wholly typical of many people's experience in the political and social world of post-war Britain. The prevalance in his poetry of moods of melancholy and disillusionment, experiences of failure and frustration, could thus be regarded as an honest depiction of the characteristic experiences of a generation.

2

There is an intimate connection between Larkin's philosophy of stoic resignation, his belief that life is inescapably meaningless, his renunciation of all striving and challenge; and his readiness to accept the common language as the appropriate medium for his verse. In 'Poetry of Departures' (*The Less Deceived*), 'ordinary life' is presented as a meaningless tidiness, repulsive in its ordinary familiarity:

> We all hate home
> And having to be there:
> I detest my room,
> Its specially-chosen junk,

> The good books, the good bed,
> And my life, in perfect order

But the images of escape from this oppressive order, images of *alternative* ways of living — excitement and adventure, fantasies of life on the open road, or before the mast — adopt the same suspicious shapeliness of form, and so cease to be real alternatives or escapes: they are 'artificial', an 'object', a 'life/ Reprehensibly perfect'. The words and images that stir the imagination of the speaker are of two kinds: the overheard remark (*'He chucked up everything'*, *'Take that you bastard'*, *'Then she undid her dress'*); and the conventional, comic-strip images of a life of adventure and excitement ('swagger the nut-strewn roads', 'Crouch in the fo'c'sle'). Both share a common characteristic: they are clichéd stereotypes of word or image, conventional and manifestly unreal.

This of course is exactly Larkin's point: the unreal perfection of the imagined life parallels the oppressive orderliness of the real. But the point is an easy one to make, when the very possibility of an alternative life is reduced to a clichéd conversational remark or a stereotypical comic-book image of adventure. The poem's language establishes, through its simple, no-nonsense diction ('We all hate home' . . . don't we? Come on, admit it!), a framework of assumptions in which the possibility of escape or alternative can appear only as superficial fantasy or fable. The poem is therefore trapped between its commitment to the common language and its ironic perception of the difficulties of escaping from the experience that language frames: it remains therefore unable to challenge or question the life the common language articulates and supports. The common language bears upon the poet with all the weight of common experience: he is imprisoned within his language as firmly as he is imprisoned within his orderly life. Where there is no attempt to re-structure language, to re-create and re-shape it into new forms of experience, there can be no effective effort to transcend or oppose a deadening, sterile, imprisoning way of life.

These observations can best be elaborated by comparing Larkin's verse with that of a very different twentieth-century poet, Dylan Thomas. Larkin's own attitude to Thomas was that of his attitude to all 'modernist' poetry — hostility, with a more immediate element of dislike, associated perhaps with a certain degree of rivalry. The essential difference between the two poets is that where Larkin is content to accept a given language, and thereby to accept the experience that language embodies, Thomas is always restlessly determined to re-shape and re-structure language into new forms, to fight through to new experiences, new feelings, new relationships. One poet takes the world and language as he finds them, and shapes them with wit, subtlety, elegance and irony; the other breaks ordinary language apart and re-composes it into a poetic challenge.

In Larkin's 'Reasons for Attendance' (*The Less Deceived*) the poet looks through a window at couples dancing. Isolated and estranged from the oblivious communal activity, he is divided between a sense of envy, and a detached contempt for the 'mass' experience; a yearning to be included, to belong, and a desire to remain separate and individual. The poem contains the characteristically easy use of colloquial speech — 'all under twenty-five'; 'Or so I fancy'; 'as far as I'm concerned'. This language is used to describe an experience of isolation and separateness; both the itching desire to participate ('The wonderful feel of girls') and the contemptuous dismissal ('they maul to and fro') are expressed in everyday phrase and diction. The poet would like to invoke a real alternative, a life of individual fulfilment, the life of 'Art'. But how can that be attempted, when the logic of the common language automatically precludes any talk of 'art' as high-flown and pretentious? And so the poet offers an apologetic and defensive, self-deprecating alternative: where the dancers are aware only of the loud jazz music, his summons is the sound of:

> . . . that lifted, rough-tongued bell
> (Art, if you like)

The confidence he feels in ordinary life and language gives him no corresponding confidence in 'art'. The ironical self-criticism of the conclusion cannot alter the basic pattern: acceptance of the common language entails acceptance of the common experiences of a particular society. If a society is alienating, isolating, frustrating, the poet who accepts its language can only *reflect* those experiences. The poet and the dancers remain for ever separate: the poet's only consolation is to doubt their happiness, to prefer, with qualified hesitation, the life of 'Art, if you like': and to mark out and establish for himself a position of wry, ironical awareness from which he can observe those 'ordinary' people with whom he identifies, and for whom he claims to write.

Dylan Thomas's poem 'In my Craft or Sullen Art' is based on the same distinction, the same separation of poet and lovers. For whom, or for what, does the poet write?

> Not for ambition or bread
> Or the strut and trade of charms
> On the ivory stages
>
> . . .
> Not for the proud man apart
>
> . . .
> Nor for the towering dead

He writes for the lovers, who 'lie abed/ With all their griefs in their arms'. The poet's art is a 'craft', involving 'labour', a 'sullen art' resistant to his efforts; yet elusive and fragile — 'those spindrift pages'. His craft is exercised 'in the still night', while the lovers in their beds may be thinking of many things, but least of all of poetry:

> But for the lovers, their arms
> Round the griefs of the ages,
> Who pay no praise or wages
> Nor heed my craft or art.

Thomas's poem is capable of the same self-deprecating irony as Larkin's; but it also insists on the *connection*, the *relationship* between himself and the lovers, his painful creativity and their moonlit, raging, grief-filled love. For Thomas, no man is truly an island: the most intimately personal experiences are, paradoxically, what link us indissolubly to one another. So the poet writes:

> . . . for the *common* wages
> Of their most *secret* heart.
> (my italics)

The paradox of isolation and togetherness, loneliness and intimacy, expresses the reality of human relationship with more truth and honesty than all Larkin's defensive irony. Essential to that achievement is the creative, exploratory use of language: although the poem has a limpid simplicity by comparison with many of Thomas's poems, it operates by means of poetic techniques which distinguish it sharply from 'ordinary' language — condensed metaphor, rhetoric, an inevitable, controlled, choreographed rhythm, quite distinct from the tentative provisionality of ordinary conversation. Where Larkin imitates, Thomas re-creates.

3

Larkin's mimetic, representational poetry is based on a characteristically English philosophy: empiricism, the basing of thought and action on observation and experiment, rather than on theory or ideas. In Larkin we find not only a lack of interest in theory, but a general distrust of ideas — either as interesting in themselves, or as part of a general theory or system of thought, whether that be philosophical, political ethical or religious. Where Larkin is concerned to address ideas, it is always in the form of a preoccupation with the traditional 'themes' of English poetry — love, time, death — and these concepts are always related to specific situations, rather than developed through argument or exposition. Ideas for Larkin have no implications beyond their immediate experiential context: so they appear in his verse only as restrictions, never as potentialities, opportunities or forces of liberation.

This 'empiricism' extends to his use of language as well as his general attitude to life: in both spheres he is content to accept and imitate the surface of life, unwilling to drive deeper into systematic thought or into new structures of language; unwilling to explore the depths and complexities of experience or of words. This limitation emerges clearly in 'Sunny Prestatyn' (*The Whitsun Weddings*). The poet observes on an advertising poster the image of a beautiful bikini-clad girl, eroticising a landscape of beaches and hotels: '*Come to Sunny Prestatyn*'. The ideal of beauty and pleasure hinted at by the poster is then defaced by obscene graffiti: 'Huge tits and a fissured crotch', 'A tuberous cock and balls', autographed with the signature of the artist, *'Titch Thomas'*. The picture of the girl is used by the poet as an image of radiant beauty, violated by the drabness and sordidness of everyday life:

> She was too good for this life

But this transcendent beauty is despoiled and ultimately destroyed by the harsh and violent realities of life: the poster disappears, to be replaced by *Fight Cancer* — 'the sour reminder' as one critic has described it 'of the pain and death of reality' (Roger Day, *Philip Larkin* — Milton Keynes, 1987–p. 29).

There seems to be no awareness within the poem of the absurdity of identifying essential beauty with an advertising image. It might well be argued, especially by women, that the exploitation of the female body is a graver offence against human values than the defacing of a poster; or that Titch Thomas's obscene emendations serve only to disclose the sexual violence that is in reality the concealed sub-text of such images. Vandalism can be regarded as a rudimentary form of social protest, and the pornographic additions as a healthy challenge to the pornographic aestheticism of the copywriter's fantasy; an insistence that the sexual lure of the poster should be seen for what it is, and that a complete conception of human experience (the comprehensive vision that we rely on poets to provide) contains its Titch Thomases as well as its idealised images of beauty.

The poem's conclusion constitutes the most powerful indictment of Larkin's empiricism, his unwillingness to probe beneath the surface. *Fight Cancer* signifies a disillusioned acknowledgement that nature can decompose and ravage the body as effectively as Titch Thomas's penknife violated the poster. All the emphasis is on *cancer*: the poet (and most of his critics) pay no attention at all to the other word, 'fight'. To 'fight' cancer is precisely to deny the necessity for resignation; to acknowledge that life contains pain and death, while refusing to accept that they cannot be opposed, combated, challenged. The fact that Larkin can regard a poster calling on people to struggle against a great life-destroyer merely as a depressing destroyer of illusion, will sufficiently indicate the limitations of his world-view and of his poetry.

4

'Lowered sights and patiently diminished expectations' lead inevitably to the contemplation of death. Larkin's poetry is distinctively incapable of making sense of the experience, of endowing death with any meaning. The simple language becomes almost abstract in its weary, inert acquiescence, its renunciation of the will:

> Life is first boredom, then fear.
> Whether or not we use it, it goes,
> And leaves what something hidden from us chose,
> And age, and then the only end of age.
>
> ('Dockery and Son', *The Whitsun Weddings*)

This too can be set beside some lines of Dylan Thomas's:

> Do not go gentle into that good night,
> Old age should rage and burn at close of day;
> Rage, rage against the dying of the light.

Thomas's poem has all the fight, the rage, the challenge that are absent from Larkin's. Thomas's poem is not at all sentimental, or consolatory, or illusioned; yet it exhorts the reader to adopt towards that most intractable of realities a more urgent and positive mode of contemplation than mere resignation, than that passive 'relapsing back' into life or into death that is the keynote of the poetry of Philip Larkin.

AFTERTHOUGHTS

1

What limitations does Holderness point to in Larkin's preference for 'common language' (pages 106–109)?

2

Explain the purpose of Holderness's comparison of Larkin's poetry with the work of Dylan Thomas (pages 109–114).

3

How justifiable do you find the criticisms of 'Sunny Prestatyn' put forward on pages 112–113?

4

Do you agree that 'passive "relapsing back" into life or into death' is the 'keynote' of Larkin's poetry (page 114)?

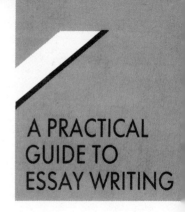

INTRODUCTION

First, a word of warning. Good essays are the product of a creative engagement with literature. So never try to restrict your studies to what you think will be 'useful in the exam'. Ironically, you will restrict your grade potential if you do.

This doesn't mean, of course, that you should ignore the basic skills of essay writing. When you read critics, make a conscious effort to notice *how* they communicate their ideas. The guidelines that follow offer advice of a more explicit kind. But they are no substitute for practical experience. It is never easy to express ideas with clarity and precision. But the more often you tackle the problems involved and experiment to find your own voice, the more fluent you will become. So practise writing essays as often as possible.

HOW TO PLAN AN ESSAY

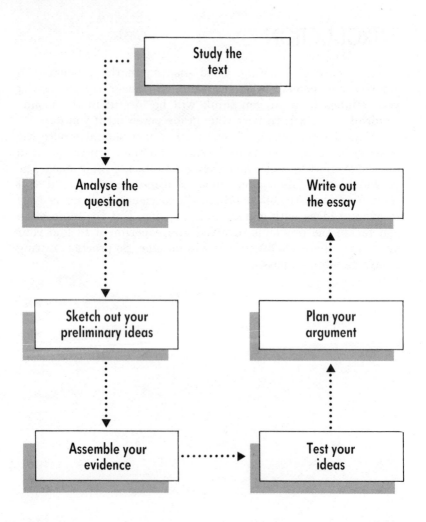

Study the
text

Analyse the
question

Write out
the essay

Sketch out your
preliminary ideas

Plan your
argument

Assemble your
evidence

Test your
ideas

Study the text

The first step in writing a good essay is to get to know the set text well. Never write about a text until you are fully familiar with it. Even a discussion of the opening chapter of a novel, for example, should be informed by an understanding of the book as a whole. Literary texts, however, are by their very nature complex and on a first reading you are bound to miss many significant features. Re-read the book with care, if possible more than once. Look up any unfamiliar words in a good dictionary and if the text you are studying was written more than a few decades ago, consult the *Oxford English Dictionary* to find out whether the meanings of any terms have shifted in the intervening period.

Good books are difficult to put down when you first read them. But a more leisurely second or third reading gives you the opportunity to make notes on those features you find significant. An index of characters and events is often useful, particularly when studying novels with a complex plot or time scheme. The main aim, however, should be to record your *responses* to the text. By all means note, for example, striking images. But be sure to add *why* you think them striking. Similarly, record any thoughts you may have on interesting comparisons with other texts, puzzling points of characterisation, even what you take to be aesthetic blemishes. The important thing is to annotate fully and adventurously. The most seemingly idiosyncratic comment may later lead to a crucial area of discussion which you would otherwise have overlooked. It helps to have a working copy of the text in which to mark up key passages and jot down marginal comments (although obviously these practices are taboo when working with library, borrowed or valuable copies!). But keep a fuller set of notes as well and organise these under appropriate headings.

Literature does not exist in an aesthetic vacuum, however, and you should try to find out as much as possible about the context of its production and reception. It is particularly important to read other works by the same author and writings by contemporaries. At this early stage, you may want to restrict your secondary reading to those standard reference works, such as biographies, which are widely available in public libraries. In the long run, however, it pays to read as wide a range of critical studies as possible.

Some students, and tutors, worry that such studies may stifle the development of any truly personal response. But this won't happen if you are alert to the danger and read critically. After all, you wouldn't passively accept what a stranger told you in conversation. The fact that a critic's views are in print does not necessarily make them any more authoritative (as a glance at the review pages of the *TLS* and *London Review of Books* will reveal). So question the views you find: 'Does this critic's interpretation agree with mine and where do we part company?' 'Can it be right to try and restrict this text's meanings to those found by its author or first audience?' 'Doesn't this passage treat a theatrical text as though it were a novel?' Often it is views which you reject which prove most valuable since they challenge you to articulate your own position with greater clarity. Be sure to keep careful notes on what the critic wrote, and your *reactions* to what the critic wrote.

Analyse the question

You cannot begin to answer a question until you understand what task it is you have been asked to perform. Re-cast the question in your own words and reconstruct the line of reasoning which lies behind it. Where there is a choice of topics, try to choose the one for which you are best prepared. It would, for example, be unwise to tackle 'How far do you agree that in *Paradise Lost* Milton transformed the epic models he inherited from ancient Greece and Rome?' without a working knowledge of Homer and Virgil (or *Paradise Lost* for that matter!). If you do not already know the works of these authors, the question should spur you on to read more widely — or discourage you from attempting it at all. The scope of an essay, however, is not always so obvious and you must remain alert to the implied demands of each question. How could you possibly 'Consider the view that *Wuthering Heights* transcends the conventions of the Gothic novel' without reference to at least some of those works which, the question suggests, have *not* transcended Gothic conventions?

When you have decided on a topic, analyse the terms of the question itself. Sometimes these self-evidently require careful definition: *tragedy* and *irony*, for example, are notoriously difficult concepts to pin down and you will probably need to consult a good dictionary of literary terms. Don't ignore, however, those seemingly innocuous phrases which often smuggle in significant assumptions. 'Does Macbeth lack the nobility of the true tragic hero?' obviously invites you to discuss nobility and the nature of the tragic hero. But what of 'lack' and 'true' — do they suggest that the play would be improved had Shakespeare depicted Macbeth in a different manner? or that tragedy is superior to other forms of drama? Remember that you are not expected meekly to agree with the assumptions implicit in the question. Some questions are deliberately provocative in order to stimulate an engaged response. Don't be afraid to take up the challenge.

Sketch out your preliminary ideas

'Which comes first, the evidence or the answer?' is one of those chicken and egg questions. How can you form a view without inspecting the evidence? But how can you know which evidence is relevant without some idea of what it is you are looking for? In practice the mind reviews evidence and formulates preliminary theories or hypotheses at one and the same time, although for the sake of clarity we have separated out the processes. Remember that these early ideas are only there to get you started. You *expect* to modify them in the light of the evidence you uncover. Your initial hypothesis may be an instinctive 'gut-reaction'. Or you may find that you prefer to 'sleep on the problem', allowing ideas to gell over a period of time. Don't worry in either case. The mind is quite capable of processing a vast amount of accumulated evidence, the product of previous reading and thought, and reaching sophisticated intuitive judgements. Eventually, however, you are going to have to think carefully through any ideas you arrive at by such intuitive processes. Are they logical? Do they take account of all the relevant factors? Do they fully answer the question set? Are there any obvious reasons to qualify or abandon them?

Assemble your evidence

Now is the time to return to the text and re-read it with the question and your working hypothesis firmly in mind. Many of the notes you have already made are likely to be useful, but assess the precise relevance of this material and make notes on any new evidence you discover. The important thing is to cast your net widely and take into account points which tend to undermine your case as well as those that support it. As always, ensure that your notes are full, accurate, and reflect your own critical judgements.

You may well need to go outside the text if you are to do full justice to the question. If you think that the 'Oedipus complex' may be relevant to an answer on *Hamlet* then read Freud and a balanced selection of those critics who have discussed the appropriateness of applying psychoanalytical theories to the interpretation of literature. Their views can most easily be tracked down by consulting the annotated bibliographies held by most major libraries (and don't be afraid to ask a librarian for help in finding and using these). Remember that you go to works of criticism not only to obtain information but to stimulate you into clarifying your own position. And that since life is short and many critical studies are long, judicious use of a book's index and/or contents list is not to be scorned. You can save yourself a great deal of future labour if you carefully record full bibliographic details at this stage.

Once you have collected the evidence, organise it coherently. Sort the detailed points into related groups and identify the quotations which support these. You must also assess the relative importance of each point, for in an essay of limited length it is essential to establish a firm set of priorities, exploring some ideas in depth while discarding or subordinating others.

Test your ideas

As we stressed earlier, a hypothesis is only a proposal, and one that you fully expect to modify. Review it with the evidence before you. Do you really still believe in it? It would be surprising if you did not want to modify it in some way. If you cannot see any problems, others may. Try discussing your ideas with friends and relatives. Raise them in class discussions. Your tutor is certain to welcome your initiative. The critical process is essentially collaborative and there is absolutely no reason why you should not listen to and benefit from the views of others. Similarly, you should feel free to test your ideas against the theories put forward in academic journals and books. But do not just borrow what you find. Critically analyse the views on offer and, where appropriate, integrate them into your own pattern of thought. You must, of course, give full acknowledgement to the sources of such views.

Do not despair if you find you have to abandon or modify significantly your initial position. The fact that you are prepared to do so is a mark of intellectual integrity. Dogmatism is never an academic virtue and many of the best essays explore the *process* of scholarly enquiry rather than simply record its results.

Plan your argument

Once you have more or less decided on your attitude to the question (for an answer is never really 'finalised') you have to present your case in the most persuasive manner. In order to do this you must avoid meandering from point to point and instead produce an organised argument — a structured flow of ideas and supporting evidence, leading logically to a conclusion which fully answers the question. Never begin to write until you have produced an outline of your argument.

You may find it easiest to begin by sketching out its main stage as a flow chart or some other form of visual presentation. But eventually you should produce a list of paragraph topics. The paragraph is the conventional written demarcation for a unit of thought and you can outline an argument quite simply by briefly summarising the substance of each paragraph and then checking that these points (you may remember your English teacher referring to them as topic sentences) really do follow a coherent order. Later you will be able to elaborate on each topic, illustrating and qualifying it as you go along. But you will find this far easier to do if you possess from the outset a clear map of where you are heading.

All questions require some form of an argument. Even so-called 'descriptive' questions *imply* the need for an argument. An adequate answer to the request to 'Outline the role of Iago in *Othello*' would do far more than simply list his appearances on stage. It would at the very least attempt to provide some *explanation* for his actions — is he, for example, a representative stage 'Machiavel'? an example of pure evil, 'motiveless malignity'? or a realistic study of a tormented personality reacting to identifiable social and psychological pressures?

Your conclusion ought to address the terms of the question. It may seem obvious, but 'how far do you agree', 'evaluate', 'consider', 'discuss', etc, are *not* interchangeable formulas and your conclusion must take account of the precise wording of the question. If asked 'How far do you agree?', the concluding paragraph of your essay really should state whether you are in complete agreement, total disagreement, or, more likely, partial agreement. Each preceding paragraph should have a clear justification for its existence and help to clarify the reasoning which underlies your conclusion. If you find that a paragraph serves no good purpose (perhaps merely summarising the plot), do not hesitate to discard it.

The arrangement of the paragraphs, the overall strategy of the argument, can vary. One possible pattern is dialectical: present the arguments in favour of one point of view (**thesis**); then turn to counter-arguments or to a rival interpretation (**antithesis**); finally evaluate the competing claims and arrive at your own conclusion (**synthesis**). You may, on the other hand, feel so convinced of the merits of one particular case that you wish to devote your entire essay to arguing that viewpoint persuasively (although it is always desirable to indicate, however briefly, that you are aware of alternative, if flawed, positions). As the essays contained in this volume demonstrate, there are many other possible strategies. Try to adopt the one which will most comfortably accommodate the demands of the question and allow you to express your thoughts with the greatest possible clarity.

Be careful, however, not to apply abstract formulas in a mechanical manner. It is true that you should be careful to define your terms. It is *not* true that every essay should begin with 'The dictionary defines *x* as ...'. In fact, definitions are often best left until an appropriate moment for their introduction arrives. Similarly every essay should have a beginning, middle and end. But it does not follow that in your opening paragraph you should announce an intention to write an essay, or that in your concluding paragraph you need to signal an imminent desire to put down your pen. The old adages are often useful reminders of what constitutes good practice, but they must be interpreted intelligently.

Write out the essay

Once you have developed a coherent argument you should aim to communicate it in the most effective manner possible. Make certain you clearly identify yourself, and the question you are answering. Ideally, type your answer, or at least ensure your handwriting is legible and that you leave sufficient space for your tutor's comments. Careless presentation merely distracts from the force of your argument. Errors of grammar, syntax and spelling are far more serious. At best they are an irritating blemish, particularly in the work of a student who should be sensitive to the nuances of language. At worst, they seriously confuse the sense of your argument. If you are aware that you have stylistic problems of this kind, ask your tutor for advice at the earliest opportunity. Everyone, however, is liable to commit the occasional howler. The only remedy is to give yourself plenty of time in which to proof-read your manuscript (often reading it aloud is helpful) before submitting it.

Language, however, is not only an instrument of communication; it is also an instrument of thought. If you want to think clearly and precisely you should strive for a clear, precise prose style. Keep your sentences short and direct. Use modern, straightforward English wherever possible. Avoid repetition, clichés and wordiness. Beware of generalisations, simplifications, and overstatements. Orwell analysed the relationship between stylistic vice and muddled thought in his essay 'Politics and the English Language' (1946) — it remains essential reading (and is still readily available in volume 4 of the Penguin *Collected Essays, Journalism and Letters*). Generalisations, for example, are always dangerous. They are rarely true and tend to suppress the individuality of the texts in question. A remark such as 'Keats always employs sensuous language in his poetry' is not only fatuous (what, after all, does it mean? is *every* word he wrote equally 'sensuous'?) but tends to obscure interesting distinctions which could otherwise be made between, say, the descriptions in the 'Ode on a Grecian Urn' and those in 'To Autumn'.

The intelligent use of quotations can help you make your points with greater clarity. Don't sprinkle them throughout your essay without good reason. There is no need, for example, to use them to support uncontentious statements of fact. 'Macbeth murdered Duncan' does not require textual evidence (unless you wish to dispute Thurber's brilliant parody, 'The Macbeth Murder Mystery', which reveals Lady Macbeth's father as the culprit!). Quotations should be included, however, when they are necessary to support your case. The proposition that Macbeth's imaginative powers wither after he has killed his king would certainly require extensive quotation: you would almost certainly want to analyse key passages from both before and after the murder (perhaps his first and last soliloquies?). The key word here is 'analyse'. Quotations cannot make your points on their own. It is up to you to demonstrate their relevance and clearly explain to your readers *why* you want them to focus on the passage you have selected.

Most of the academic conventions which govern the presentation of essays are set out briefly in the style sheet below. The question of gender, however, requires fuller discussion. More than half the population of the world is female. Yet many writers still refer to an undifferentiated *man*kind. Or write of the author and *his* public. We do not think that this convention has much to recommend it. At the very least, it runs the risk of introducing unintended sexist attitudes. And at times leads to such patent absurdities as 'Cleopatra's final speech asserts *man*'s true nobility'. With a little thought, you can normally find ways of expressing yourself which do not suggest that the typical author, critic or reader is male. Often you can simply use plural forms, which is probably a more elegant solution than relying on such awkward formulations as 's/he' or 'he and she'. You should also try to avoid distinguishing between male and female authors on the basis of forenames. Why *Jane* Austen and not *George* Byron? Refer to all authors by their last names unless there is some good reason not to. Where there may otherwise be confusion, say between T S and George Eliot, give the name in full when it first occurs and thereafter use the last name only.

Finally, keep your audience firmly in mind. Tutors and examiners are interested in understanding your conclusions and the processes by which you arrived at them. They are not interested in reading a potted version of a book they already know. **So don't pad out your work with plot summary.**

Hints for examinations

In an examination you should go through exactly the same processes as you would for the preparation of a term essay. The only difference lies in the fact that some of the stages will have had to take place before you enter the examination room. This should not bother you unduly. Examiners are bound to avoid the merely eccentric when they come to formulate papers and if you have read widely and thought deeply about the central issues raised by your set texts you can be confident you will have sufficient material to answer the majority of questions sensibly.

The fact that examinations impose strict time limits makes it *more* rather than less, important that you plan carefully. There really is no point in floundering into an answer without any idea of where you are going, particularly when there will not be time to recover from the initial error.

Before you begin to answer any question at all, study the entire paper with care. Check that you understand the rubric and know how many questions you have to answer and whether any are compulsory. It may be comforting to spot a title you feel confident of answering well, but don't rush to tackle it: read *all* the questions before deciding which *combination* will allow you to display your abilities to the fullest advantage. Once you have made your choice, analyse each question, sketch out your ideas, assemble the evidence, review your initial hypothesis, plan your argument, *before* trying to write out an answer. And make notes at each stage: not only will these help you arrive at a sensible conclusion, but examiners are impressed by evidence of careful thought.

Plan your time as well as your answers. If you have practised writing timed essays as part of your revision, you should not find this too difficult. There can be a temptation to allocate extra time to the questions you know you can answer well; but this is always a short-sighted policy. You will find yourself left to face a question which would in any event have given you difficulty without even the time to give it serious thought. It is, moreover, easier to gain marks at the lower end of the scale than at the upper, and you will never compensate for one poor answer by further polishing two satisfactory answers. Try to leave some time at the end of the examination to re-read your answers and correct any obvious errors. If the worst comes to the worst and you run short of time, don't just keep writing until you are forced to break off in mid-paragraph. It is far better to provide for the examiner a set of notes which indicate the overall direction of your argument.

Good luck — but if you prepare for the examination conscientiously and tackle the paper in a methodical manner, you won't need it!

Poem titles in quotation marks. Titles of poetry collections are given in italics. In a hand-written or typed manuscript this would appear as underlining e.g. <u>The Less Deceived</u>.

Short verse quotations incorporated in the text the essay within quotation rks. If the quotations ran to a second line of poetry, his would be indicated by a slash (/).

the happy aggression of this ceremonial shot into the future ('arrow-shower') merging imperceptibly with the fertility and procreativeness of 'rain'. It is a happy vision for the spectator-poet, but we should still notice that this liberating event is '*somewhere* becoming rain'. 'Somewhere' is not so desolate a word here as it is in 'Sad Steps', but its spatial vagueness still has the power to exclude: neither the poet nor the wedding-crowds have a place in the ultimate fulfilment.

Despite these exceptions, however, Larkin's poetry is dominated by the longest perspective of all: death. And in event he is not the spectator, not the accidental sharer helpless co-participant in the universal private bleakest, most uncompromising expression of it con late poem, 'Aubade'.[2]

Long verse quotation indented and introduced by a colon. Quotation marks are not needed. The poem from which the quotation is taken should be given in brackets at the end of the quotation or (as here) specified in the preceding text.

dication ootnote

> . . . I see what's really always there:
> Unresting death, a whole day nearer now,
> Making all thought impossible but how
> And where and when I shall myself die.
> Arid interrogation: yet the dread
> Of dying, and being dead,
> Flashes afresh to hold and horrify.

In an interview Larkin once remarked, 'I can only say I dread endless extinction.' The remark is very precise, and all I wish to do here is to stress these two dominant aspects of Larkin's fear of death: extinction and endlessness. This is the nature of his 'long perspective': the human journey from being to not-being, from time to timelessness, from place to vacancy. In the second stanza of 'Aubade', he specifies his dread in just this way:

Three dots (ellipsis) dicate where words or ses have been cut from otation or when (as here) quotation begins mid-sentence.

> . . . the total emptiness for ever,
> The sure extinction that we travel to
> And shall be lost in always. Not to be here,
> Not to be anywhere,
> And soon; nothing more terrible, nothing more true.

short prose quotation incorporated in the text of the essay, within quotation marks.

Death for Larkin is dissolution, oblivion and emptiness. The long perspective of death both enhances the value of precarious

---

[2] First published in *The Times Literary Supplement*, 23 December 1977.

otnote, supplying iographical information as specified on pages 132 - 133.

We have divided the following information into two sections. Part A describes those rules which it is essential to master no matter what kind of essay you are writing (including examination answers). Part B sets out some of the more detailed conventions which govern the documentation of essays.

PART A: LAYOUT

Titles of texts

Titles of published books, plays (of any length), long poems, pamphlets and periodicals (including newspapers and magazines), works of classical literature, and films should be underlined: e.g. David Copperfield (novel), Twelfth Night (play), Paradise Lost (long poem), Critical Quarterly (periodical), Horace's Ars Poetica (Classical work), Apocalypse Now (film).

Notice how important it is to distinguish between titles and other names. Hamlet is the play; Hamlet the prince. Wuthering Heights is the novel; Wuthering Heights the house. Underlining is the equivalent in handwritten or typed manuscripts of printed italics. So what normally appears in this volume as *Othello* would be written as Othello in your essay.

Titles of articles, essays, short stories, short poems, songs, chapters of books, speeches, and newspaper articles are enclosed in quotation marks; e.g. 'The Flea' (short poem), 'The Prussian Officer' (short story), 'Middleton's Chess Strategies' (article), 'Thatcher Defects!' (newspaper headline).

Exceptions: Underlining titles or placing them within quotation marks does not apply to sacred writings (e.g. Bible, Koran, Old Testament, Gospels) or parts of a book (e.g. Preface, Introduction, Appendix).

It is generally incorrect to place quotation marks around a title of a published book which you have underlined. The exception is 'titles within titles'; e.g. 'Vanity Fair': A Critical Study (title of a book about *Vanity Fair*).

Quotations

Short verse quotations of a single line or part of a line should be incorporated within quotation marks as part of the running text of your essay. Quotations of two or three lines of verse are treated in the same way, with line endings indicated by a slash(/). For example:

1   In Julius Caesar, Antony says of Brutus, 'This was the noblest Roman of them all'.
2   The opening of Antony's famous funeral oration, 'Friends, Romans, Countrymen, lend me your ears;/ I come to bury Caesar not to praise him', is a carefully controlled piece of rhetoric.

Longer verse quotations of more than three lines should be indented from the main body of the text and introduced in most cases with a colon. Do not enclose indented quotations within quotation marks. For example:

It is worth pausing to consider the reasons Brutus gives to justify his decision to assassinate Caesar:

> It must be by his death; and for my part,
> I know no personal cause to spurn at him,
> But for the general. He would be crowned.
> How might that change his nature, there's the question.

At first glance his rationale may appear logical . . .

Prose quotations of less than three lines should be incorporated in the text of the essay, within quotation marks. Longer prose quotations should be indented and the quotation marks omitted. For example:

1   Before his downfall, Caesar rules with an iron hand. His political opponents, the Tribunes Marullus and Flavius, are 'put to silence' for the trivial offence of 'pulling scarfs off Caesar's image'.
2   It is interesting to note the rhetorical structure of Brutus's Forum speech:

> Romans, countrymen, and lovers, hear me for my cause, and be silent that you may hear. Believe me for my honour, and have respect to mine honour that you may believe. Censure me in your wisdom, and awake your senses, that you may the better judge.

Tenses: When you are relating the events that occur within a work of fiction or describing the author's technique, it is the convention to use the present tense. Even though Orwell published *Animal Farm* in 1945, the book *describes* the animals' seizure of Manor Farm. Similarly, Macbeth always *murders* Duncan, despite the passage of time.

PART B: DOCUMENTATION

When quoting from verse of more than twenty lines, provide line references: e.g. In 'Upon Appleton House' Marvell's mower moves.'With whistling scythe and elbow strong' (l.393).

Quotations from plays should be identified by act, scene and line references: e.g. Prospero, in Shakespeare's The Tempest, refers to Caliban as 'A devil, a born devil' (IV.1.188). (i.e. Act 4. Scene 1. Line 188).

Quotations from prose works should provide a chapter reference and, where appropriate, a page reference.

Bibliographies should list full details of all sources consulted. The way in which they are presented varies, but one standard format is as follows:

1 Books and articles are listed in alphabetical order by the author's last name. Initials are placed after the surname.
2 If you are referring to a chapter or article within a larger work, you list it by reference to the author of the article or chapter, not the editor (although the editor is also named in the reference).
3 Give (in parentheses) the place and date of publication, e.g. (London, 1962). These details can be found within the book itself. Here are some examples:

>   Brockbank, J. P., 'Shakespeare's Histories, English and Roman', in Ricks, C. (ed.) English Drama to 1710 (Sphere History of Literature in the English Language) (London, 1971).
>   Gurr, A., 'Richard III and the Democratic Process', Essays in Criticism 24 (1974), pp. 39–47.
>   Spivack, B., Shakespeare and the Allegory of Evil (New York, 1958).

Footnotes: In general, try to avoid using footnotes and build your references into the body of the essay wherever possible. When you do use them give the full bibliographic reference to a work in the first instance and then use a short title: e.g. See K. Smidt, <u>Unconformities in Shakespeare's History Plays</u> (London, 1982), pp. 43–47 becomes Smidt (pp. 43–47) thereafter. Do not use terms such as 'ibid.' or 'op. cit.' unless you are absolutely sure of their meaning.

There is a principle behind all this seeming pedantry. The reader ought to be able to find and check your references and quotations as quickly and easily as possible. Give additional information, such as canto or volume number whenever you think it will assist your reader.

SUGGESTIONS FOR FURTHER READING

Works by Larkin

Poetry
Larkin's four major poetry collections — *The North Ship* (1945), *The Less Deceived* (1955), *The Whitsun Weddings* (1964) and *High Windows* (1974) — are printed along with much previously unpublished material in *Collected Poems*, ed. Thwaite, A (London, 1988)

Fiction
Jill (London, 1946)
A Girl in Winter (London, 1947)

Non-fiction
All What Jazz: A Record Diary 1961–68 (London, 1970)
Required Writing: Miscellaneous Pieces 1955–82 (London, 1983)

Critical studies of Larkin's writing
Day, R, *Larkin* (Milton Keynes, 1987)
Motion, A, *Philip Larkin* (London, 1982)

Essay collections, combining personal memoirs with commentary
Chambers, H (ed.), *An Enormous Yes* (Peterloo Poets, Calstock, Cornwall, 1986)
Hartley, G (ed.), *Philip Larkin 1922–1985: A Tribute* (London, 1988)
Salwak, D (ed.), *Philip Larkin: The Man and his Work* (London, 1989)

Longman Group UK Limited
*Longman House, Burnt Mill, Harlow, Essex, CM20 2JE, England
and Associated Companies throughout the World.*

First published 1989
ISBN 0 582 03810 3

*Set in 10/12 pt Century Schoolbook, Linotron 202
Printed in Great Britain by Bell and Bain LTD., Glasgow*

Acknowledgements

We are grateful to the following copyright holders for permission to
reproduce poems:

Faber and Faber Ltd for 'High Windows' and extracts from 'To the Sea',
'The Old Fools' and 'Show Saturday' in *High Windows* by Philip
Larkin, 'Love Songs in Age', 'Faith Healing' and extracts from 'Refer-
ence Back', 'MCMXIV', 'Send No Money', 'An Arundel Tomb', 'The
Whitsun Weddings', 'Naturally the Foundation will Bear Your
Expenses', 'Mr Bleaney', 'Ignorance', 'Self's the Man', 'Dockery and
Son', 'Nothing To Be Said' and 'Water' in *The Whitsun Weddings* by
Philip Larkin; The Marvell Press for 'Wires' and extracts from 'Born
Yesterday', 'Reasons for Attendance', 'Wedding-Wind', 'Coming',
'Poetry of Departures', 'Church Going' and 'Dry-Point' in *The Less
Deceived* by Philip Larkin; Times Newspapers Ltd for extracts from
'Aubade' by Philip Larkin, first published in *The Times Literary
Supplement* 23.12.77.